TRUE GRIT

D0377487

TRUE GRIT

Women Taking on the World, for God's Sake

by Deborah Meroff

Authentic

LONDON • ATLANTA • HYDERABAD

Copyright © 2004 Deborah Meroff

12 11 10 09 08   13 12 11 10

Reprinted 2004, 2005, 2006 (4)

First published 2004 by Authentic Media
9 Holdom Avenue, Bletchley, Milton Keynes, Bucks, MK1 1QR, UK
285 Lynnwood Avenue, Tyrone, GA 30290, USA
OM Authentic Media, Medchal Road, Jeedimetla Village,
Secunderabad 500 055, A. P., India
www.authenticmedia.co.uk

Authentic Media is a division of Send the Light Ltd., a company
limited by guarantee (registered charity no. 270162)

The right of Deborah Meroff to be identified as the Author of
this Work has been asserted by her in accordance with the
Copyright, Designs and Patents Act 1988.

All rights reserved. No part of this publication may be
reproduced, stored in a retrieval system, or transmitted in any
form or by any means, electronic, mechanical, photocopying,
recording or otherwise, without the prior permission of the
publisher or a licence permitting restricted copying. In the UK such
licences are issued by the
Copyright Licensing Agency.
90 Tottenham Court Road, London, W1P 9HE

British Library Cataloguing in Publication Data

A catalogue record for this book is available from the
British Library

ISBN 1-85078-575-9

Cover Design by Sam Redwood
Printed and bound in the US by Versa Press

Contents

Introduction

This book may disturb you. While collecting the facts included in *True Grit* over these many months, I have been shocked, saddened, outraged. Many excellent publications are already available about particular wrongs faced by today's women. My purpose is to give the reader a quick overview of them all, a simplified guide that will lend itself to ready reference. Hopefully, this type of presentation will also motivate more readers to action.

For the Christian, the first and most obvious and powerful response is intercession. The 'Vital Statistic' files should act as a starting point. They are not meant to be comprehensive; in most cases they only touch on the situation in a selection of countries. The Appendices suggest books and websites for further exploration.

I hope that many readers will also choose some of the other action options. I have noted a few organizations that are working to combat some of the horrors facing girls and women. Every voice, every letter of protest, every bit of support will help to win these campaigns.

The women 'on God's search and rescue team' chosen for this book are not superstars. They were chosen because they have the same ordinary fears and failings we all experience.[1] And while none of these women felt they could take on the world, each one has been willing, by God's grace, to tackle one small corner of it. Take encouragement, as I have, to see what can happen when, as Mother Teresa put it, they simply allowed themselves to become 'pencils in the hand of a writing God, who is sending love letters to the world.'[2]

Just a word of warning. Passionate prayers not only change the world, they have a way of transforming the people who pray them. As God channels his concern for the world through you, you may find yourself moving out in unexpected ways. This should not come as a surprise. God's goal is to recruit every one of us for his search and rescue team!

Debbie Meroff

Notes

1 The women's names in chapters one, two, five, six and seven have been changed for identification purposes.
2 Original source unknown.

Chapter 1

Breaking the silence

'Blindness separates people from things;
deafness separates people from people.'
Helen Keller

Kathryn Bridges stood quietly in front of the historic Wailing Wall: the last remains of Jerusalem's ancient temple, and sacred to all Jews. As usual, both the men's and women's sections were crowded. Some visitors sat on chairs, praying; others stood touching the Wall itself. A few wept, pushing into the cracks of the sun-bleached stones a written cry from the heart, to join the thousands already there.

Kathryn suddenly became aware of a man and young girl standing not far away. Their distinctive clothing suggested they were ultra-orthodox Jews, and while she watched she saw them silently 'speak' together in signs. When they happened to glance her way she smiled, and gave the universal signal to communicate that she, too, was deaf. Immediately they began to converse.

During the next hour the distance between the strangers was bridged as Kathryn 'listened' to the pair express their discouragement. Week after week they faithfully attended the synagogue without being able to understand what was being said. The comfort of the messages was lost to them, for rabbinical law ruled that signed translation should not be permitted on the Sabbath. Signing was considered 'work'.

The plight of this father and daughter saddened Kathryn's heart. She understood all too well the pain of being cut off from 'normal' people's conversations. But to also be refused the privilege of entering into worship with others in the name of religion seemed unnecessarily cruel. For Kathryn, serving and worshipping the Lord her God was more important than life itself.

It had been that way ever since she was nineteen. At that point in her life, death had seemed like a welcome alternative to a future holding endless misery, both for herself and her family. Her father was a proud farmer who had never really accepted having a profoundly deaf daughter. But when she reached the age of two and a half, something remarkable happened. Christians who knew the family prayed for the little girl, and 35 per cent of her hearing was suddenly restored. No physiological explanation was ever found. But little Kathryn now had enough hearing, with aids, to learn how to speak.

For the next twelve years she was able to communicate with a world that had previously held only silence. Sounds came alive; the voices of those she loved. A barking dog. Music.

And then, for no apparent reason, the window of hearing abruptly slammed shut once again. Isolated by silence at fourteen, and no longer able to cope with a normal public school, Kathryn was sent far away to a boarding school for the deaf to finish her education. The experience left her traumatized. The school was run by nuns who enforced harsh discipline on the students. Kathryn finally returned home with a bruised and bitter spirit.

By this time a major social crisis had erupted in her country. Race riots everywhere were threatening to tear whole communities apart. While Kathryn, her mother and brother held the same opinion about the government's responsibility, her father took the opposite view. Discord within the household grew until one night it reached an explosive climax. Kathryn's father pulled out a gun and started firing. She and the others fled for their lives.

For the next weeks, the three lived in temporary housing. The teenager's depression deepened as she blamed herself for her father's hatred. Perhaps, she thought, it would be better for everyone if she ended it all. Gradually a plan evolved. But when the day arrived to take the overdose, she had an unexpected encounter. An acquaintance persuaded her to meet at a coffee bar. It was a Christian coffee bar, and the strangers she met – warm, happy and not deaf – welcomed her as a friend. As she lay on her bed that night, thinking about what had happened, she suddenly heard an urgent internal voice telling her to get out of bed and pray.

Kathryn was astonished. She didn't even know how to pray. All she could remember were the rote prayers she had memorized at boarding school. But the voice persisted. She slipped out of bed and onto her knees.

'Lord, please help me!' she whispered. 'I believe you are there.' As she waited a tide of inexpressible peace began to course through her, covering all the hurt and hopelessness of the past. With a wonderful certainty she knew that God had heard her. And he was reaching out to heal.

The fact that Jesus had loved her enough to intervene in such a personal way overwhelmed Kathryn. She gave her life into his keeping, and in so doing gained the self-confidence she had always lacked. She began to make plans for a career in civil engineering. During university she came into contact with many more of the deaf Christian community. Sign language had always been strictly forbidden while she was growing up. Those who signed just made themselves 'conspicuous', and even less likely to be accepted by the 'normal' world, or so her parents told her. As a result Kathryn could only lip read. But now, learning to use her hands to communicate, exciting new possibilities opened up.

After graduation, Kathryn's life fell into a happy routine of work, church fellowship and friends. Some of the believers she met were actively involved in evangelism and missions, but this never really seemed like an option to her. Being deaf provided the perfect excuse. One day, however, she was reading some verses in Exodus chapter four. The words God spoke to Moses stabbed her heart: 'Who gave man his mouth? Who makes him deaf or mute? Is it not I, the LORD? Now go, I will help you speak and will teach you what to say' (verse 4).

Impossible as it seemed, she knew the command to 'go' was for her. The Lord was directing her to dive off the deep end. So Kathryn signed up for a month-long outreach with Operation Mobilization. She surprised herself by emerging triumphantly. But this was only the beginning.

Kathryn spent the next year in further training for missions. Gradually, seeds that had been planted many years before began to grow in her heart. She remembered the Jewish speech therapist that had persuaded her mother to send her to a Jewish school when she was small. These had been happy days, and she had even kept in touch with some of her friends, many of whom had since emigrated to Israel. Kathryn found herself thinking more and more about serving God in that country. Yet the idea terrified her. How could she ever cope in a strange place, where people spoke another language and where she couldn't even lip read? She decided to throw herself on God's mercy and sent in her application.

About this same time an Israeli family arrived at the OM office to give a few months' training to the recruits. The timing couldn't have been coincidental. This family answered Kathryn's questions about Israel, encouraged her and prayed with her. When leaders accepted her application, she knew it was a green light from God. The practical support that came from many unexpected sources during the next months was added confirmation.

Although Kathryn had braced herself for the shock of changing cultures, she was not prepared for the fear, frustration and terrible loneliness that engulfed her those first days and weeks in Israel. The promise that God would never leave her or forsake her became a reality throughout. His voice was a lifeline throughout her first year of studying Hebrew and Hebrew sign language.

Kathryn was startled to discover that Israel's sign vocabulary was still relatively undeveloped. A committee was in place to expand the number of terms, especially as new words like 'computers' and 'stereos' were constantly being added to the ancient Hebrew. But virtually no signs existed for Christian terms such as 'redeemer,' or 'salvation.' Even the usual sign for 'Jesus,' touching the palms of the hands to denote nail prints, was offensive to Jews.

What was she to do? She couldn't create new signs on her own but how else was she to communicate her faith? As a bridge between the deaf and hearing worlds, she had a unique opportunity.

The next five years were a steep learning curve. Research showed there were around 28,000 deaf residents in the country. Of that number she found only a few who were Christians. To her joy, several new friends that she made among the deaf community also came to know Jesus through her testimony.

But the pioneer ministry team she gathered around her was pitifully inadequate. A few hearing women joined her from other countries, learned how to sign in Hebrew, and provided invaluable backup. A deaf male friend from Tel-Aviv sometimes helped. Yet it became increasingly obvious that more deaf Christians with some Hebrew knowledge would be essential for the work to proceed.

One of Kathryn's first moves was to link the scattered deaf believers in the country with a bi-monthly Bible study. She hoped this fellowship would one day develop into the first deaf Messianic congregation, a spiritual 'home' with its own pastor. An informal club for deaf and hearing also began to meet in the women's flat every week. Occasional practical courses in subjects like knitting and cooking were introduced. Then flannel-graph visuals were donated to the team, as well as equipment for making Bible study videos. The fellowship dreamt of renting space for a small activity centre, where friends could feel free to drop in at all hours.

Sadly, many of the aids available to deaf people in other countries had not yet found their way into Israel in the 1990s. Hearing dogs were unknown, as were text phones and telephone relay services. Visual alarms for doorbells were too expensive to import. Deaf young people were only just beginning to access computers and e-mail communication. Those who could afford them used fax machines. And the only signed programme on Israeli television was the eleven o'clock news. Although subtitled films were occasionally offered, a lot of the older deaf community couldn't read.

In more recent years, Israel's disabled residents have increasingly communicated their anger at the government's failure to address problems. Some have demonstrated in front of the Parliament building, demanding benefits that will help them integrate better into the hearing society. Although a small number of deaf clubs have started, not everyone can afford to pay the membership fees necessary to keep them going.

Kathryn knows from personal experience that even in the western world, many still look upon the deaf as mentally deficient. Deaf children are sometimes given only limited educational opportunities. But at least the disabled can get jobs and even travel abroad. In much of the Middle East such things remain a dream. Deaf people are often unemployed and deprived of any means to better their situation.

How could Kathryn begin to face the challenge? She ached to reach out to those who had no hope. Meeting with the orthodox father and daughter at Jerusalem's Wailing Wall sustained that vision. How could she find ways to reach more members of the deaf orthodox community?

Teaching computer skills to members of a club for the deaf at a university provided one way of deepening relationships. She often met up with students at the university café and talked with them before classes.

One week, classes were cancelled to allow students to go on an outing with the deaf club. A suicide bomb went off in the university café around the same time they usually met, killing and wounding many men and women. Kathryn and her computer students were stunned. But for the grace of God, they might have been among the victims.

Terrorist attacks, shootings and bombings still continue to add to the daily stress of Israeli life. For the deaf it's

even worse. The simple act of crossing the street can be
hazardous for someone who cannot hear a police siren or
fire engine. But riding a bus along the Bethlehem border,
where two other buses on the same route have been
blown up, Kathryn refuses to allow the uncertainties to
roadblock God's purposes. She is now teaching computer
classes four times a week at a deaf club, and English
classes once a week. Home and hospital visits to friends
and contacts are also a vital part of her ministry. And the
monthly Bible studies in Hebrew sign language have
proven such a source of fellowship that Kathryn wants to
start a similar group for deaf Arab believers.

Yet daily administrative tasks still clamour for
attention. Sending prayer updates and information,
important as that is, is time-consuming. Printing out and
practising songs for the monthly deaf Bible studies and
finding more visual aids for those who can't read are also
daily chores. Income to buy resources is inadequate.
Money is needed for a vehicle to transport people to
meetings. But staff is the biggest concern. Volunteers and
visitors do what they can, but committed long-term team
members are needed to meet all of the opportunities.

One priority continues to be recruiting and training
hearing Israeli believers as interpreters. During her first
years in the country Kathryn had not found a single
church fellowship that offered interpretation in Hebrew
sign language. How could fellowships hope to attract or
minister to the deaf community? Deaf believers are like
trees that are cut off, she explains with passion. They
cannot grow without help. So, added to her other com-
mitments are private classes in Hebrew sign language,
for hearing believers who are willing to be interpreters.

The desert of need stretches far beyond the borders of
Israel. All over the Middle East, intermarriage within
families has led to an abnormally high incidence of

handicapped individuals. Approximately ten million suffer from deafness. Yet comparatively little has been done to improve their quality of life. What can be done to reach them?

But first, Kathryn has to scale the wall in front of her. As it is, feelings of inadequacy sometimes threaten to overwhelm her. How, for instance, can she presume to minister to men and women who have endured the horrors of the Holocaust? One deaf man confided how he had survived the death camps as a boy only by pretending that he could hear. Eighty-four-year-old Anya, who emigrated to Israel from Russia, described the day that a Christian Bible had saved her life.

'When Nazi soldiers murdered friends, I was alone. Standing among the bodies, I was too terrified and shocked to move. Then I noticed a Bible on the ground and bent to pick it up. When they found me holding the Bible, they assumed I was a Christian. Then they let me go.'

Anya lost that Bible, but someone later replaced it with a picture version. Although she didn't read well, she often looked at the illustrations.

One day Kathryn invited Anya to watch a video about Jesus in sign language. As the story unfolded, the old woman was visibly moved. How, she wanted to know, could deaf people talk to God? Kathryn gladly explained that God had no trouble understanding sign language; he even knew the thoughts within every heart. At the end of the video, Anya signed the prayer of salvation along with the Russian interpreter. The eighty-four-year-old entered into the joy of a new life in Christ.

Kathryn Bridges has not suffered the same traumas as some of the Jewish people she works with. Yet she, too, is a survivor. Thanks to the grace of God, the hurt and misunderstandings of her past have given her empathy for others well beyond her years.

Kathryn now thinks of Israel as home and hopes to keep living and ministering in the country permanently. Like any young woman she also dreams of a husband and a family. But whatever direction the future takes, the Lord is her strength and song. And although the rest of the world may be silent she is content, as long as his voice leads her on.

VITAL STATISTICS: The hearing impaired

Approximately 250 million people have a severe hearing impediment. More than two-thirds live in the Third World. Seventy million are completely deaf or have only a minute hearing capability. Over 80 per cent of these people have no access to education.

- The deaf are the fourth largest people group in the world who are unreached with the gospel.
- Ninety per cent of the deaf have hearing parents. Only about 1 in 10 of these parents can communicate with their child in sign language.

WORLDWIDE ESTIMATES OF HEARING IMPAIRED POPULATIONS BY REGION

Region	Estimates (millions)
Africa	22
North America	31
South America	18
Central America	2
South East Asia	112
Caribbean	2
Europe	30
Far East	90
Middle East	10
Australasia	1
Total	318

Source: *World Book of Facts*, (Funk & Wagnall: Mahwah, New Jersey, 1995) cited on {http://www.deafworldministries.com}.

The top three countries with hearing impaired populations are:

China	73 million
India	90 million
USA	23 million

In the **United States** the deaf community are listed by several mission agencies as the largest unreached people group in America. The native language of deaf people here, American Sign Language (ASL) is the **third most used language** in North America. Fewer than **8 out of every 100** deaf people ever attend church. Fewer than **4 out of 100** claim a personal relationship with Christ.[1]

Each year, nearly 10,000 women and children become permanently deaf due to being repeatedly struck on or near the ear.[2]

In a survey of 245 women with disabilities by the Disabled Women's Network of **Canada**, 40 per cent had experienced abuse; 12 per cent had been raped. Perpetrators of the abuse were primarily spouses and ex-spouses (37 per cent) and strangers (28 per cent), followed by parents (15 per cent), service providers (10 per cent) and dates (7 per cent). Less than half these experiences were reported, due mostly to fear and dependency.

Abuse of women with disabilities is an issue of epidemic proportions worldwide.

SPECIAL PROBLEMS OF ABUSED DEAF WOMEN

- Dealing with police, court systems, shelters and other support services is made more difficult because of the few people who understand sign language.
- Deaf women suffer higher unemployment rates and lower salaries than most.
- Economic dependency on others often leads to being trapped in abusive situations longer.
- Guilt, shame and low self-esteem often influence deaf women to suffer without protest.

Notes

1. See Silent Blessings website: {http://www.silentblessings.org/}.
2. Deaf Women Against Violence, 24802 Mission Blvd., Hayward, CA, 94544 USA.

VITAL STATISTICS: Childbirth

- Only 65 per cent of women in developing countries receive antenatal care during pregnancy.
- It is estimated that more than 90 per cent of people alive today were born at home. Each year, 60 million babies are born without a trained midwife present.
- Bolivia has the highest maternal death rate in pregnancy throughout all of Latin America. Only a quarter of women in country areas have medical help during labour. In India about 30,000 women die each year during and after childbirth; 140 women die as a result of childbirth in Britain.
- According to the World Health Organization, as few as 5 per cent of women receive care after their baby is born in very poor countries and regions. By contrast, 90 per cent of new mothers in developed countries receive postnatal care.
- Sixteen hundred women die every day, some only in their teens, from causes related to childbirth. Of these, 99 per cent are in the developing world. While the maternal death rate in Canada is only 1 in 7300, in Africa it is 1 in 12.

MOST COMMON CAUSES OF DEATH DURING PREGNANCY AND CHILDBIRTH

Cause	Death (thousands)
Haemorrhage	125
Self-attempted abortion	55
Infection	75
Convulsions	60
Obstructed Labour	40

Source: *World Health Organization*, Fact Sheet no. 276, February 2004.

Three million have died from one or more of these causes since 1990.

Complications

- Although they survive, 50 million more women each year suffer complications that leave humiliating, painful and long-term infections, injuries and disabilities.
- One factor contributing to the high incidence of obstructed labour in the developing world is early marriage. Girls can be ten or even younger, which means they give birth when their pelvis is too small. This can result in permanent nerve damage and muscle deterioration in the feet and legs. Those worst affected become crippled.
- In some parts of Arab West Africa, midwives insert a long knife into an overly narrow vagina. This can do terrible damage to the bladder or rectum. Sometimes the knife is inserted down the urethra to make the cut, laying bare the entire lower urinary tract. Many women die immediately from haemorrhage.
- An estimated 80,000 women yearly are left with fistula after obstructed labour. This is the rupturing of bladder and rectum resulting in permanent incontinence. Few women can afford surgical repair. In addition to the embarrassment and shame, folklore in some areas proclaims obstetric fistula to be the result of marital infidelity or sexually transmitted disease. Girls and young women suffering from fistulas are ostracized by their communities and abandoned by their families. Many are forced to become beggars.
- A cleansing ritual practiced by some African cultures can also cause fistula. For 40 days following childbirth, a friend or relative pours a solution containing potash into the mother's vagina. If the solution is improperly made the alkali causes chemical destruction of the vaginal tissue, and a fistula develops.

Chapter 2

Over the rainbow

'Live to love. Love to live.'
Amy Carmichael

Tammy Koh was a businesswoman. She had worked hard to get where she was and had paid for it with a gastric ulcer. So where did it come from, this certainty that God wanted her to leave Singapore for the far-away kingdom of Nepal?

Life for Tammy had not got off to a very promising start. Her early years had been overshadowed by her mother's obsessive compulsive behaviour disorder, behaviour that had driven her father to become physically abusive. A normal home was almost impossible. Mrs Koh practised rigid rituals that everyone else had to follow, like walking on only one side of the room, or turning on the tap in a certain way. Tammy and her younger sister often heard explosions of anger between their parents. The situation deteriorated until she was nine, when her mother came to her school to tell her that she was leaving their father. The little girl watched her leave in heartbroken shock, tears raining down her face. Would she ever see her mother again? What was to become of her and her sister?

Mr Koh took the two girls to live with his sisters and mother. Tammy bridled whenever they made derogatory remarks about her mother, doing her best to defend her. The oddly assorted family moved several times, adding to the sisters' feeling of rootlessness. One of their aunts ran a brothel. Tammy was aghast when the day came that her cousins were sent to work in the business. Were she and her sister destined for the same fate?

Eventually Mrs Koh contacted the girls and they were able to meet occasionally, in secret. She confided that she was living in a small room and saving money so that one day they could live together again. But their father found out about the meetings. Drunk and enraged, he fell on the girls and beat them brutally. Tammy found herself being picked up and hurled to the floor.

'Who do you want to live with?' he shouted, 'me or your mother? Choose!'

Tammy's terrified sister stuttered that she would stay with him. But Tammy shook her head. She wanted to go and live with her mother.

With a roar of anger her father promptly dragged his cut and bleeding daughter out of the house. When the two got to a cemetery he reached into his pocket and threw a few dollars at Tammy.

'If you want your mother,' he told her, 'you should just take off and find her. I don't want anything to do with you anymore. I'm finished!'

Tammy sobbed as he swore once more and staggered off.

For the second time she had been abandoned by a parent. After what seemed a long time, a passing stranger took pity on the child and helped her find her mother's address.

For the next few years, Tammy lived with her mother and grandmother in a cramped apartment. Her sister eventually came to join them. But Tammy's hatred for her father continued to simmer, occasionally erupting in rebellion. As a teenager she earned a reputation for fighting with friends and family alike. Relations with her elderly grandmother were especially volatile. One day when she was fourteen they had a particularly bitter quarrel. Tammy admitted to a friend that she had a problem with her temper, and he confided how his own life had changed after giving himself to Jesus. The Koh family were strong Buddhists or Taoists,[1] and Tammy didn't like being disloyal to the ancient traditions. But she was desperate. She prayed, confessed her sins and invited Christ to take control of her mixed-up emotions.

On the surface, nothing changed very dramatically. But the hatred that had eaten away at Tammy for so long mysteriously vanished. She was astonished that she could even discover feelings of pity for her father. The next time he visited them, about a year later, tears came to her eyes. She knew there was no logical explanation for her change of heart and realized it was proof of God's healing touch. The family even tried to live together again for a while, although it didn't work out.

Mrs Koh was pleased to observe the change in her rebellious daughter. Her approval switched to anger, however, when Tammy explained that she had become a Christian. To the older woman this was a betrayal of everything that was Chinese. Tammy knew that as the eldest child she was expected to carry out religious duties, such as the veneration of ancestors. Mrs Koh forbid her attendance at church and tried to cut her off from Christian friends. Tammy was forced to read her Bible secretly and forsake any fellowship. But when her sister also accepted Jesus into her life a year later, their mother lost control. She grabbed a knife and held it threateningly to Tammy's throat. The girls had to choose what they wanted most: Jesus Christ or life.

Courageously, both sisters told her they would be true to Jesus, whatever the consequences. Mrs Koh didn't carry out her threat, but the tension at home became more and more unendurable. When Tammy was seventeen, their mother finally ordered both girls to leave.

Tammy was already used to working hard. She had been helping to support herself since she was fourteen, employed in a paper factory during school holidays and weekends. Her quick, logical mind helped her achieve high marks at school, however, and she was determined to graduate from high school. She dreamt of studying mathematics at college. But for two years she had little time for anything except making ends meet for herself and her sister.

The girls had never sought a rift in their relationship with their mother.

'If mother ever asks us to return, we will, for Christ's sake,' they agreed.

It was not a decision they made lightly. The woman's neurotic behaviour was still a great source of misery for everyone around her. But Mrs Koh did eventually relent. Her daughters moved back in, making it clear that they must be allowed to attend church.

Tammy eventually gained her college degree. She and her sister started a small gift shop and then, after taking an accounting course, she began another company that offered financial services to individuals. Her faith remained important to her. But at a missionary conference one time, listening to a story of missionaries being martyred for the sake of the gospel, she questioned the extent of her commitment. By the end of that conference she made a silent decision to follow God into missions if he should call. Then his voice spoke to her heart: 'If you have made the decision to respond, why don't you stand up for *me*?'

Tammy started to tremble. What if she was just imagining the voice? With great courage, she stood to make her commitment public. The trembling was replaced by certainty.

Several more years passed. Tammy was twenty-seven and managing two thriving businesses when she took some time off to attend a mini-World Missions Expo in Malaysia – a 'Direction Camp' organized by Operation Mobilization.

The camp confronted her with an unexpected challenge. It had never before occurred to her that bookkeepers and business people might be used to advance God's Kingdom. But now she was hearing about many fields that were urgently in need of this type of expertise. Was God trying to tell her something? She prayed that if he wanted her to respond, he would show her where and when before she left the camp. In the next days she began to feel a pull in her heart towards Nepal.

Tammy was at that time attending a fledgling Christian fellowship. Attendance was still very small. So when she returned from the conference and announced that God was leading her in the direction of Nepal, she did not expect the few dozen people there to do more than pray for her. But they surprised Tammy. The fellowship committed itself to fully meeting her field expenses. Later, the mother church volunteered to take over Tammy's support.

Another heavy financial obligation remained, however. Children in her culture were expected to support their parents in old age. Tammy and her sister felt that if God were truly sending her to Nepal, they would have to trust him to meet this need as well.

In 1996 Tammy flew out to Kathmandu to begin the most challenging and fulfilling chapter of her career. The Nepali culture and lifestyle were very different from home. Years of stress had given Tammy a gastric ulcer, and the hot, spicy and oily foods in her new diet did not, at first, appeal to her. But soon she was able to swallow the dahl and rice and lentil soup with no ill effects – in fact, the ulcer completely healed! She also found herself enjoying the comfortable Punjabi suits worn in that part of the world.

But although Kathmandu was surrounded by stunning Himalayan scenery Tammy was quick to realize that life for most Nepalis was far from ideal. The capital city lay in a valley that was congested and polluted. The people who lived there wrestled daily with unemployment, poverty, and alcohol addiction. By any standards, Nepal was one of the world's poorest countries. Over half of the population survived on less than one US dollar a day. Only about 15 per cent of homes had electricity.

On almost every street where Tammy walked she saw shrines dedicated to the gods of Hinduism. The only hope for the vast majority of Nepalis was that their next reincarnation would be a better one. As she worked in the office her first year, her compassion grew. Particularly for the women.

One of the women she met confided that she had once lived in a village outside Kathmandu with her husband and child. Dilu's husband turned out to be an abusive alcoholic who plainly cared more for another woman than his own. One day, in a drunken stupor, the man poured kerosene over their son, intending to set him ablaze. Dilu and the boy managed to escape injury, but her husband later abandoned them. The destitute pair travelled to the city to find employment. By the time Tammy came into their lives, even that hope had faded. Their situation was desperate.

Dilu tried to describe a dream that had come to her, about earning money with a shop. Tammy decided she would help. She found a small room for the woman and her son to live in, and paid for her training as a seamstress. Dilu still had no income, so Tammy asked her to make a few articles that she could buy as souvenirs. Dilu produced so many items that she began to try selling them to other people. Suddenly, the demand exceeded the supply.

Dilu was finally able to make her benefactor understand that her dream was not about making money in her own shop. It was about Tammy starting a sewing project that could help many troubled women like herself.

The vision captured Tammy's imagination. She had been horrified to learn that over a third of Nepali girls were married off by the age of sixteen; in the villages some were even made to marry at eleven or twelve. Many husbands later abandoned the girls and married again somewhere else. Parents who arranged the marriage might take responsibility and receive their daughter back. But if it was a love match, the girl was blamed. She was expected to fend for herself and her children whatever way she could.

Even in cases of rape in the village, female victims were often the ones held responsible. They, not the perpetrators, were imprisoned, even if they were pregnant. Inheritance laws were also unfair, dictating that only men could inherit property.

Tammy remembered the old proverb, 'Give someone a fish and you feed them for a day. Teach them to fish, and you feed them for life.' Most Nepali girls were unprepared for any vocation besides homemaking. The practical solution for helping abandoned women was to train them for a job that would provide ongoing support, not only for themselves but for their children.

In 1997, with the aid of Christians back in Singapore, Tammy set up a few sewing machines in her home and invited several needy women to make simple items for sale. The craft business they started soon earned enough to allow expansion into its own premises. Knitting classes also began. Ten sewing machines allowed thirty women to make colourful shoulder bags, backpacks, purses, spectacle holders and other items of Nepali material and design.

Most of the workers were wives of alcoholics or single mothers. A few girls had been abducted as children to serve as sex slaves in various Indian brothels. Release for victims like these usually only comes when they contract Aids or another fatal illness. And families rarely take them back. Tammy's goal was not only to give these women a means of support, but to heal the terrible psychological scars. Vocational training gave them a sense of dignity. Some employees were eventually able to start their own businesses.

Tammy looked into other income-generating projects to help more women, and came up with soap-making. Again, supporters in Singapore backed her with start-up funds, and production got underway in 2000. The 100 per cent natural handmade soaps proved to be a hit in Nepal's tourist shops. The handicraft business had more local competition, requiring Tammy to seek an ever-widening base of sales outlets overseas to keep the business profitable.

So many women applied for vacancies that occurred in the workshops that Tammy had to screen each person carefully. While wanting to assist as many as possible, she limited the numbers so that each worker could be sure to receive her personal attention. Obviously, this wasn't just a business enterprise. Tammy was concerned for the emotional, physical and spiritual well-being of each woman. Often she visited them in their homes.

In some cases, workers called themselves Christians but they were far from closely walking with the Lord. Other women knew little about Jesus Christ. Sangeeta's story was sadly typical. Her family forced her into marriage with a man forty-eight years older than herself, who had had five previous wives. The man proved to be a wife-beater and an alcoholic. Eventually he sold Sangeeta's only source of income – a knitting machine – to pay for drink. When her husband finally died at the age of eighty-one, he left her with four small boys and debts that amounted to the staggering sum of ten thousand dollars. In her despair, Sangeeta found Jesus Christ. But years of abuse in Kathmandu had broken her spirit. She saw little hope of a future for herself or her sons until she was accepted into the soap-making programme. Now her outlook is completely different. Her faith has been rekindled.

Lydia was also a victim of sorts. As a little girl, Lydia was made to drink the blood of an animal offered to idols. Ever since that day she has been tormented by epileptic seizures. As her family was too poor to buy medicine to control her disease, Lydia was often injured or burned when she fell into the fire. She had no prospects for marriage or employment. But when Tammy gave her a job, she was able to buy the medicine she needed. Lydia's life changed drastically. Allowing God into her heart changed it even further. Today her face is radiant – still scarred on the outside, but reflecting the healing within.

Helping battered mothers naturally led to doing something for their deprived children. A generous donor gave Tammy and her team the funds to kick-start a 'Child Education Program'. This has assisted in paying school fees and buying the uniforms required for education in Nepal. Some children also receive medical and food assistance. In cases where the father is an alcoholic and the mother feels unable to cope, the team finds a temporary foster home for children.

One widowed mother Tammy met had four children, two of them with cerebral palsy. The mother was earning barely enough to cover their house rental. But as a Hindu idol worshipper she still faithfully bought food to offer her idols. The team started visiting this family, bringing along basic food items. Eventually the woman and her children were invited to the team house for a hearty meal. Afterwards they watched the Jesus film together.

The next time Tammy visited the family, she was astonished to find that the idols had vanished from the house!

'I have decided to put my trust in Jesus,' the mother told her.

Soon, the whole family was going to church.

The combination of Tammy's hard-headed business acumen and warm-hearted sensitivity was a recipe for success. But she often experienced feelings of inadequacy. As a single woman she had never had to cope with an abusive partner or dependent children. The practicalities of running the workshops were also stressful. Workers occasionally denied the truth or argued if they were confronted with a sub-standard job. Deception occurred. Satan used every ploy he could to dishearten Tammy or derail the project.

Then in 2002, he pulled out all the stops. Two former staff members conspired to duplicate Tammy's soap formula, with the intention of taking over her sales outlets. The betrayal hurt deeply. Damaging lies about her business were also circulated. Negative publicity appeared in a newspaper, the journalist making claims that her soap was being sold at exorbitant prices, and that workers were fired unless they agreed to become

Christians. Officials investigated and interrogated the staff.

By October the situation had deteriorated to the point that Tammy's visa was in jeopardy. A few weeks later, she was ordered to leave the country.

A shattered Tammy retreated to Singapore. She wrote to friends: 'I want to thank God for his comfort and protection. I have learned to be more dependent on him, and understand now the suffering Jesus went through when he was betrayed or abandoned by his disciples.'

Her greatest concern was for the women she'd left behind – the workers with whom she had shared laughter and tears, disappointments and triumphs. They attempted to struggle on without their leader but it was difficult. Tammy fought her case, meanwhile doing all she could to widen the market for her soap and craft products. A trip to another Asian country revealed the possibility of starting a similar business there, to help orphans.

On the personal side, her relationship with her mother improved to such an extent that Mrs Koh even supported her wish to return to Nepal. And then came the most unexpected breakthrough of all: the joy of leading her father to the Lord.

After four months, the Nepal court made the unprecedented decision to reinstate Tammy's visa. She was free to return and resume her work.

Tammy still marvels at the way God has redeemed the bitter experiences of her life. She would never have considered herself a likely vessel for pouring out his love and grace. But he turned her own abused childhood into a deep compassion for women in the Mountain Kingdom of Nepal; and then gave her the tools to help them back to wholeness. Even her temporary exile had resulted in good. When the 'all clear' came through, Tammy was reminded of her heavenly Father's promise: 'See, I have placed before you an open door that no-one can shut. I know that you have little strength, yet you have kept my word and have not denied my name' (Rev. 3:8).

Tammy hopes that one day she can hand over the whole business to Nepali management. She maintains that it belongs to God. And although her heart is still in the Himalayas, she is ready to obey if the Lord should send her elsewhere, perhaps to start more such projects in neighbouring countries.

Tammy's horizons have widened considerably. She has learned the hard way that taking risks is part of the adventure of serving God. And that beyond each storm is a rainbow beyond imagination.

Notes

1 Taoism is a philosophy advocating non-interference in natural events, supporting magic and superstition.

VITAL STATISTICS: Nepal

- It is estimated that twelve women die every day in Nepal as a result of pregnancy. Half of these deaths are abortion related, although abortion is illegal. *Nepal's maternal mortality rate is among the highest in the world.*[1]

> **Nepal also has one of the lowest female literacy rates. Girls average 39 per cent; boys 61 per cent. Less than 25 per cent of women have basic literacy skills.**

- Studies show that girls between the ages of ten and fourteen work twice as many hours as boys in the same age group and often do much heavier labour.[2]
- Over 62,000 children under the age of fourteen are used as domestic workers in the cities.

> **A third of Nepali girls under the age of sixteen are married. Of this, 7 per cent become wives under ten and 40 per cent marry before they are fourteen.**

A few years ago, the *Kathmandu Post* ran a story about a woman in her late thirties about to give birth to her eighteenth baby. Sansari Bhujel was married at eleven and started having children at thirteen. Nine of her children have died from malnutrition; one girl was married off at fourteen, and the remaining seven live in hunger and sickness.[3] While the number of live births in this case is unusual, child marriages resulting in high infant mortality is not.

- An estimated 200,000 Nepali women and girls have been kidnapped or sold by destitute parents into India's brothels, forced to work as prostitutes. The trade is increasing, with between 12,000 and 40,000 more trafficked every year. Buyers can obtain girls for as little as 4 dollars and sell them to brothels for 1500 dollars.

Around 20 per cent of victims are under sixteen. Some girls are as young as ten. When girls contract Aids, as a high number do, they are discarded. So are any HIV-positive babies.

'O Lord, how long will you look on? Rescue my life from their ravages, my precious life from these lions.' Ps. 35:17

Notes

1 Keshab Poudel, 'Killing Mother', {http://www.nepalnews.com} vol. 23, no. 17, November 14th–20th 2003.
2 'Facts about Girls in Nepal,' CWIN Nepal, {http://www.cwin-nepal.org/press_room/factsheet/fact_girls.htm}.
3 'Mother of 17, Sansari looks forward to her 18th baby', Kulchandra Neupane, *Kathmandu Post*, 19th Nov 2001, p.1.

VITAL STATISTICS: Child labour

At least 250 million of the world's children – one out of six – work for a living. Nearly half of them put in the same hours as adults. Two-thirds endure hazardous conditions.

Little girls make particularly popular employees because they can be paid less than anyone. Domestic service is probably the largest and most hidden employer of under-age girls worldwide.

Africa

Forty-eight million children work in sub-Saharan Africa. In all of Africa, about two out of five children earn some kind of income.

- *Morocco's 'Little Maids'*: Between 14,000 and 20,000 small girls have been sent from the countryside to work as domestic servants in private homes, in Casablanca alone. The International Labor Organization estimates there are a total of 50,000 girls in service all over Morocco – some as young as five and six. These children have become targets for abuse, often made to labour 16 hours a day, sleep on the floor and eat only scraps. Two-thirds have to work even when they are ill. Some girls have been chained up when their employers go away for the weekend. Others have been starved to death, burned with irons, or raped and thrown on the streets when they become pregnant. The small amount of pay they earn goes to their fathers. A government hotline receives some 1000 calls a week about child maids in distress. Although the government prohibits forced labour, it does not effectively enforce it.[1]

Parents in Fez, Morocco, are paid 10–12 dollars per month for their five-year-old daughters' labours at carpet factory looms. Between 5000 and 10,000 children aged eight to fourteen work in the carpet industry.

- *West Africa:* Children as young as three years old are being exploited as domestic and agricultural workers in several countries. Some parents 'lease' their offspring to Arab Gulf states, Lebanon and Europe for as little as 15 dollars. Traffickers promise children, many who are orphans, with quality schooling and vocational training abroad. In September 2001, a boat ferrying hundreds of trafficked girls sank off the coast of Cameroon, killing nine. Other cases document girls being treated as virtual slaves, forced to work day and night peddling goods in the market, fetching water and caring for young children. Most endure beatings and psychological abuse, including death threats and warnings that they will never see their parents again. Girls who escape sleep on the street, knock on the doors of churches, or accept invitations into the homes of strangers. Some are driven into prostitution and become victims of Aids.[2]

A child slave market has flourished for years in one of the popular shopping areas of Abidjan, **Ivory Coast**. Wealthy local women go there to buy their domestic help.

EUROPE

- Around 3000 **Albanian** children are trafficked to **Italy** and **Greece** in order to earn money begging and cleaning car windows for their adult 'masters'.[3]

ASIA AND PACIFIC

Sixty-one per cent of child workers under fourteen (127 million) live in the Asia Pacific area.

'Procurers' typically promise destitute parents that they will give their children a good job and education in the city. Other children are kidnapped to work in factories and sweat shops. Most receive no pay and are confined in squalid living conditions, beaten with sticks and iron rods and not allowed to see their parents. Children have been discovered branded with red-hot irons, burned with cigarettes, starved, whipped, beaten while hanging upside down, chained up, sexually abused and kept locked in cupboards for days on end.[4]

- *Bangladesh:* Almost a third of the country's children are working to help their families survive. The government estimates about 6.6 million are aged five to fourteen.
- *India:* Children, requiring only a fraction of the salary paid to adults, form a significant part of the work force in the manufacture of *beedi* (small cigarettes), matches, jewellery, carpet and cotton rope-making, domestic work, quarrying, mining and farming. Reliable agencies estimate between **75 and 115 million** children under the age of fourteen are working. And although all bonded labour and servitude was officially abolished in 1975, at least 15 million children today are 'bonded' to pay back family loans. These are the ones most exploited and abused. Many are made ill by harmful conditions or exposure to chemicals. Poor pay and inflated interest rates make it almost impossible for loans to be repaid.

'My sister is ten years old. Every morning at seven she goes to the bonded labour man, and every night at nine she comes home. He treats her badly; he hits her if he thinks she is working slowly or if she talks to the other children, he yells at her. He comes looking for her if she is sick and cannot go to work. I don't care about school or playing. I don't care about any of that. All I want is to bring my sister home from the bonded labour man. For 600 rupees[5] I can bring her home – that is our only chance to get her back. We don't have 600 rupees . . . we will never have 600 rupees.'
    Lakshmi, nine-year-old cigarette roller in Tamil Nadu.[6]

- *Pakistan:* There are 10 to 15 million child-workers, with at least 8 million of them under the age of fifteen. Debt bondage enslaves 7 to 8 million children, but authorities at national and provincial levels continue to ignore the problem. Even though bonded labour has been a punishable offence since 1992, no one has ever been prosecuted for breaking the law.
- *Philippines*: Around 5 million children work, 60 per cent in highly hazardous workplaces sometimes for 16 hours a day.
- *Indonesia:* Seven-hundred thousand under-age children are put to work as domestics.
- *Australia:* According to a report in 2000, 70,000 children under sixteen work for the clothing industry up to 20 hours or more a week alongside their immigrant parents. The children, as young as eight, work in poor conditions in homes and backyard sweatshops, and are exposed to hazards. An average of 1600 children aged between twelve and sixteen are seriously injured, maimed or killed each year in industry.

LATIN AMERICA
About 7 per cent of the world's child workers between the ages of five and fourteen live in Latin America. One in six children there are wage earners. More than 2 million are being sexually exploited, with a growing number of sex tourists going to Central America.

- *Mexico:* Eight out of ten children start working before the age of fourteen. About 3.5 million between the ages of six and eighteen work regularly.

NORTH AMERICA
- UNICEF reports that at least 100,000 children are believed to be involved in commercial sexual exploitation.

'Arise, cry out in the night . . . pour out your heart like water in the presence of the Lord. Lift up your hands to him for the lives of your children, who faint from hunger at the head of every street.' Lam. 2:19

Notes

1 Elizabetta Anna Coletti, 'Little Maids of Morocco', *Los Angeles Times*, 16th September 2001.
2 Human Rights Watch report, April 2003, 'Borderline Slavery: Child Trafficking in Togo'.
3 Global March, CRCA, *The Vicious Circle*, 2000.
4 'Child Slaves of South Asia', Anti-Slavery Society.
5 The equivalent of approximately 17 dollars.
6 Interview in Human Rights Watch report, September 1996.

Chapter 3

At home on the sea

'Joy is not the absence of trouble, but the presence of Christ.'
E. Trueblood

Joy Yorba was five years old when her life turned an abrupt corner. Like so many families in America, hers came apart with her parents' divorce. Joy lived with her mother but in time got a new dad. A plumber by profession, her stepfather took various construction jobs, which meant the family moved around a lot from one town to another. By the time she graduated at eighteen, Joy had attended thirteen different schools, and only two of them for as long as two years.

But one of her early memories was of her grandparents taking her to Vacation Bible School. Learning Bible stories and verses were a steadying anchor. When she was about ten, the family returned to live with her grandparents. Their small community happened to have a church with a very good pastor who had originally planned to go into missions. The Christian novels and missionary stories he gave Joy made a deep impression, and she accepted Jesus Christ into her life. Happily, her stepfather also became a

Christian around the same time, and her mother returned to the faith she had once had. From then on, wherever the family moved they looked for the best Bible-teaching church in town.

Life changed again after Joy's stepfather trained as a deep-sea diver in order to qualify for underwater repair of oil pipelines. In 1970 an assignment took him and his family to Singapore. They were still living there in 1971 when the Operation Mobilization ship *Logos* tied up for the first time. Seventeen-year-old Joy went to visit the book exhibition along with her classmates, and found the floating ministry fascinating. The former Danish vessel was manned by 130 young men and women from many countries, all committed to serving God. Little did Joy imagine, at that point, that she would one day be joining them.

A new contract the next year took the family to the Gulf state of Dubai for three months. To their surprise the *Logos* turned up again, and because there weren't many westerners in the country, Joy's family were invited to the official opening in Dubai. She and her sister found themselves getting 'hands on' involvement in ship life, this time as volunteer dishwashers! The experience gave them practical insight into what the ministry was really about. What really impacted them was the amount of time the crew devoted to prayer.

Dave Thomas, the ship's second engineer from England, also made a positive impression. Joy listened to him speak at a mission hospital in the neighbouring state of Sharjah, and liked what she heard. She also warmed to his friendly way with other people.

Even as a child Dave Thomas had dreamed of going to sea. He trained as a marine engineering cadet, and later, because he was a Christian, joined up with a team who were praying for a mission ship. Operation Mobilization purchased the ship in 1970, and Dave sailed as an engineer. All that he needed to complete his happiness now was a partner. After meeting the dark-haired American girl in Sharjah, he sensed she was the one.

Joy's stepfather finished his contract in the Gulf and most of the family moved to Belgium to spend the next year working with OM. Joy returned to the States and got a job there, living with her father until she had decided what to do next. Meanwhile she began to exchange letters with Dave on the *Logos*. Dave and Joy came to know each other very well through their correspondence during the next eighteen months. When they met up again in England in 1974, it was for their wedding.

Dave had taken a year off from the *Logos* to earn his chief engineer's ticket, intending to get the required commercial experience on a cargo carrier. Fortunately, now that he was married, his bride was allowed to accompany him. Even so, Joy was not expecting to spend the rest of her life at sea. She and Dave were considering a ministry in Bangladesh. OM had a few small boats there and Dave had done some relief work, driving in truckloads of aid supplies. He and Joy decided to buy a van they could outfit with furniture, in preparation for going out to live in the subcontinent.

After Dave secured his chief engineer qualifications, the couple went to the States to visit Joy's family and celebrate their first wedding anniversary. There they received a phone call from OM's ship office. Was there was any chance they would consider joining the *Logos*, instead of going to Bangladesh? The ship was in critical need of an engineer with Dave's credentials. Joy and Dave agreed. The van went out to Bangladesh that year without them.

Setting up a new home on the *MV Logos* required some ingenuity. Their cabin measured only seven feet by ten feet, with just enough space for a bunk (which could be pulled out to double the size at night), a sink and small closet. Toilets and showers were communal.

On her very first voyage from Bombay to Bari, Italy, the awful truth dawned that Joy was prone to seasickness. During the year with Dave on the cargo ship she had not suffered at all, even though they had sometimes sailed for over a month at a time. But the vast size of that vessel had lent it stability. And as she was to learn, the longer you are at sea, the easier it is for the body to adjust.

The *Logos* was by contrast only eighty-two metres long and under fourteen metres wide. She had also been designed as an icebreaker, and the shape of her hull tended to hit the waves the wrong way. Not only did the vessel pitch and roll, she corkscrewed – a nauseating combination of both movements. Joy was miserable from the moment the *Logos* got underway. She even got sick if the ship was tied up in an unprotected port, rocking in heavy swells.

But since everyone on the ship had a practical work assignment, Joy was determined to do her share. Each morning at six she turned up faithfully to help prepare the crew's breakfast and wash dishes. The dining area of the *Logos* doubled as a conference room for public meetings, so it was always a rush to clear away after meals. Later on she and the other wives divided up cleaning and laundry duties. But Joy and Dave always managed to find time together to walk on the quayside and explore new ports-of-call.

Going off the ship was almost the only way to ensure some privacy. The couple not only shared their floating home with 130 staff and crew-members, but hundreds and sometimes thousands of visitors. Every day men, women and children queued up to attend conferences and visit the book fair. The little ship throbbed with life from the moment her gangway was lowered at the end of each sail, from early morning to late at night. With a world two-thirds covered by water, using a ship to reach people with the gospel made sense. In fact, the idea was proving so successful that OM was in the process of acquiring a second ship.

Joy and Dave were delighted when they learned that they, too, were increasing: Joy was pregnant. But her pregnancy was traumatic. The ship's doctor confined her to bed for weeks, and even when she was back on her feet she was limited to non-physical work in the finance office. Her refusal to take seasick tablets because of the baby added to her discomfort. Joy and Dave decided to leave the ship in Italy, so that Joy could give birth in England. Little Christopher came safely into the world in July 1976, and twelve days later they rejoined the ship in Scotland.

For a while the family lived with the same cabin situation as before. Later they moved to the chief engineer's cabin, which boasted a separate office for Dave and the luxury of their own small bathroom. The sleeping area was so tiny that Christopher, and later their second son John, slept on the floor behind a toy box in the adjoining office.

The ship sailed to Marseille and then made its way to Mombassa, East Africa. By the time they reached the Red Sea it was the hottest time of the year. Christopher, now fifteen months old, was feverish with tonsillitis. The ship had very limited air conditioning so each time the fever rose, Joy cooled him down in a cold bath. But to their horror Christopher suffered two episodes of convulsions. Later they were to learn that this was a hereditary tendency. Christopher's convulsion threshold was so low that doctors kept him on anti-convulsion medication until he was about seven.

In 1978 Joy and David rejoiced at the birth of their second son on board the ship in the Philippines. John David was the second baby ever to be born on the ship. His delivery was premature, however, and at some point he didn't receive enough oxygen. Unaware of the problem, the family were not too concerned with John David's slow development. Various check-ups in Korea and Hong Kong did not signal any alarm. But when the family went on leave to England later that year, their family physician made an appointment with a consultant. The specialist's verdict confirmed the worst: John David had cerebral palsy.

The hospital's medical staff urged Joy and David to remain in England so the baby could be enrolled in the best physical therapy programme. The family committed themselves to staying as long as necessary. Dave found a job, and every six months during the next few years they saw the consultant. By two and a half John David was doing so well that he was able to go into the normal school system. But very soon afterwards, he fell ill with viral pneumonia. Normally this would have settled in the lungs. In John David's case it went to his most vulnerable area: the brain. Just three days later the little boy was gone.

Devastated, Dave and Joy sought to comfort each other. Doctors warned that with her medical history, Joy should not contemplate another pregnancy unless she was under the constant care of a specialist. Should they adopt? Experts recommended that they try for a child younger than Christopher, who was by then five years old. They applied, but no child was available. With this option blocked, they decided after much prayer to trust God for another child of their own. Joy put herself in the hands of a specialist and twenty months after losing John David, gave birth to a healthy baby daughter, Heather, in 1982.

Dave wound up his contract with Sealink Ferries and the family rejoined the *Logos* in France. For the next five years Heather and Christopher knew no home but the sea, sailing thousands of miles around Europe, the Americas and the Caribbean.

Their sleeping quarters were adjacent to the chief engineer's, with a hole cut through the wall of their parents' cabin. By day the ship ran a nursery that allowed mothers the freedom to do other jobs. Joy cleaned the engineers' accommodation section where her family lived, and ran the crew library.

Mothers had to be inventive to keep their older 'sea urchins' from running wild after school. Joy started a craft club and science club for the children. When Christopher was older, he also became a member of the Boy Scouts that his aunt oversaw in America. He was able to link up with Scouts in several different Latin American countries after this. It proved a real aid to learning Spanish. Christopher's fluency in later years meant that he spent many summers doing evangelistic outreaches in Spain.

Both children enjoyed the little ship school, taught by well-qualified teachers. Seasickness held no horrors for them, but they saw no problem in occasionally praying that their teachers would be sick enough to give them the day off! The pair invented all kinds of games, running up and down the hallways to follow the surge of the waves.

Christopher and Heather saw crew-members as part of their family. Often they participated in programmes for the public. International nights, featuring national costumes and music from around the world, were a highlight in every port. Films and conferences also encouraged local churches, and helped to introduce Jesus to audiences of all ages. Teams going on shore visited schools, hospitals and prisons, and held open-air programmes.

Christopher grew to be a sturdy little boy: in his element when allowed to accompany a ministry team with his father and other men from the engine department. Dave often loaded up a projector and drove off with the crew to some unreached destination to screen the *Jesus* film. The whole family, of course, routinely participated in Sunday teams to local churches. These usually offered interesting glimpses and tastes of foreign cultures. Joy still remembers trying a soup in Korea that contained noodles, eggs and ice cubes. The Philippines offered *balut*, a fertilized duck egg with a partially developed duckling, eaten boiled. And in Turkey everyone enjoyed *doner kebabs*. Dave's stomach was stronger than Joy's, but as she was smaller she could always offer the explanation that she didn't eat much.

Living on a ship definitely meant having to plan ahead for holidays. Back in the 1980s, packages from home never seemed to arrive at all. Contents had to be listed on the outside, and customs inspectors often decided they needed the articles more than the recipients. Even if families did think to buy Christmas and birthday presents in advance, there wasn't much space for storing them in cabins.

Meals on the ship were prepared and served by dining room staff. While this saved time, the menu could sometimes get tiresome. Married women were allowed to use the galley or kitchen once a month for private baking. When Dave held monthly engine room parties, Joy and the other engineer wives provided a much-appreciated feast.

By the second half of 1987 the *Logos* was making her way down the western coast of South America. Adding to Joy's usual seasickness was an inner ear problem that sometimes made her so dizzy she couldn't move her head or even eyes. The only bearable option was absolute stillness. Initially, the imbalance hit her only every few years. Later it was every six months. With the help of doctors she learned to recognize the signs and take medication whenever it flared up.

The end of the year found the ship's family spending a happy Christmas in Punta Arenas, Chile. The children were thrilled with a close-up visit to penguins in a nearby national park. Fellowship with the local churches was welcoming. Some of the huge crowd that attended the ship's Christmas-Around-the-World programme were led to their first true celebration of Jesus' birth. Then the ship sailed to her last port-of-call on the Pacific side of the continent, the southernmost town in the world: Ushuaia, Argentina. Joy was in charge of official receptions and remembers that Dave and other English crew-members were warned to be sensitive about the Falkland Islands issue. But for Dave and his team of special project workers, the highlight of the port was the completion of a new accommodation section. This was the culmination of many months' work, and families were eagerly anticipating a move to better quarters.

On January 4th the *Logos* set out on the Beagle Channel. Following this route, the ship could reach the Atlantic side of South America without going around the extreme tip. But on the first evening they ran into a Force Eight gale. Joy and most everyone else who wasn't working took seasick tablets and retired early to bed. Dave was in the engine room.

Shortly before midnight, the pilot asked the captain's permission to disembark. His pilot boat was alongside the *Logos*, communicating its intention to return to port because of the bad weather. If the pilot didn't leave with it, then he would be stuck on the ship for the remainder of the four-day voyage to the next port.

Since the *Logos* had almost reached the end of the Beagle Channel, the captain granted the pilot's request.

Dave awaited the all clear after the man climbed down the rope ladder, planning to join Joy as soon as possible.

But back in her cabin, a sudden violent trembling of the ship jolted Joy awake. She immediately sensed that the *Logos* had run up on something solid. Jumping out of bed she rushed to gather her sleeping children into her own cabin. Christopher was by this time eleven-years-old, and Heather, five.

Within moments her fears were confirmed: the ship had gone onto the rocks. Dave told Joy he expected they could de-ballast the *Logos*, lightening her enough to move off the ledge. They could then take her to the nearest port for repairs. But what no one realized was that the keel of the vessel had snapped. She was destined never to move off the rocks.

Two crew-members were stationed outside Joy's cabin to assist her. Every once in a while, one of them went to get the latest information. Their cabin also had an audio hook-up to the dining room, where the rest of the ship's company had assembled. All through that long night Joy could hear them pray, sing and claim the promises of Scripture. Although some wept, most were confident that God would redeem the little ship that had served him for so many years.

Meanwhile, the crew worked to lighten the *Logos* even as the storm continued throwing her against the rocks. Just before dawn, the ship was holed. Water began pouring into the damaged hull. Everyone was ordered to report immediately to lifeboat stations.

Joy had always kept an emergency bag of extra clothing in the same place as their life jackets. When she heard the order to abandon ship she grabbed Chris' shoes – still drying out after a camping trip, along with the other things – and hustled the children up to the boat deck. One of the men carried Heather.

At the lifeboat station she was relieved to find Dave waiting. Unsurprisingly, however, he stayed with his family only long enough to see them safely onto a Chilean navy vessel that had responded to the accident signal. Then he and the first mate went back to the stricken *Logos*. The rest of the staff and crew were transported to a navy base called Puerto Williams – the most southerly Chilean settlement before Antarctica. Joy, Christopher and Heather spent the night with one of the Navy families, while most of the single people slept in the schoolhouse. The next day the majority were flown back to Punta Arenas. Listed crew members remained behind with the captain for the official inquiry. Only Dave and the First Mate kept a vigil on the *Logos*.

Joy was still in a state of semi-shock. She had never expected events to end this way. Even when everyone abandoned ship she thought they would somehow manage to get the vessel off the rocks, and into port. They would at least be able to go back and retrieve their personal belongings. But only in Punta Arenas did she fully grasp how far the ship was from help: they would never see their floating home again.

For Dave, in a way, the loss was far worse. He had given everything to the *Logos* since the very beginning of her ministry, often working a fourteen-hour day, six days a week. The shipwreck was almost like losing another child. When he re-boarded the vessel it must have been tempting to take away his family's possessions. Their cabin was still above the waterline. But he felt it wouldn't be fair; the rest of the crew did not have the same opportunity. He only rescued Heather's pet hamster. And he and the captain removed the papers and documents needed from the bridge. Eventually, salvage rights to the *Logos* were signed over to the Chilean Navy.

Dave later admitted that he would have grabbed the photograph albums if he had thought of it: they contained the best pictures of all three of their children. But fortunately, Joy and Dave had made a practice of sending their family films back to his parents. After developing them they would forward the photos and keep the negatives. As albums on the ship got full they also sent these back to his parents. So in all they lost only about three months' record of their travels. Thanks to one of the Chilean naval officers who boarded the foundered ship, they also eventually received some of the family pictures that had been hanging on the wall.

In Punta Arenas, believers all over the city opened their homes to care for the shipwrecked crew and staff. Churches also collected used clothing and sacrificially provided for every need. When Dave ultimately showed up still wearing his boiler suit, he very gratefully exchanged it for 'civilian' wear. After several days, most of the staff and crew were flown to a Bible College in Buenos Aires until everyone's travel details could be sorted out.

The Thomas family flew from Chile to England, stopping en route in California for about three weeks. Joy remembers her sense of disorientation after landing in prosperous America and going shopping at K-Mart. She struggled to think of the dozens of things they needed to replace. Once back in England they stayed in Dave's hometown of Gillingham, borrowing the unoccupied house of a church couple. By early February they were resettled and the children were back in school. They remained there all the next school year as well, while a replacement ship was found and refitted. Dave spent most of his time in a Netherlands shipyard and returned home for a long weekend every month. Sometimes they joined him during school holidays. But at long last, in June 1989, they moved as a family onto the refurbished *Logos II*.

It was an emotional day for them all. For twelve-year-old Christopher and seven-year-old Heather, it meant getting back to normal. Life on a ship was no deprivation but a constant source of educational, social and spiritual adventure. Heather had found the English lifestyle too confining! Even though the family lived in a huge house she couldn't just run out of the front door and visit friends, because of the constant stream of traffic. On the ship she was safe to roam anywhere.

The children now had their own cabins adjacent to their parents'. Along with a few other primary-aged children on board, Heather attended a school on the deck beneath the book hold. Joy supervised Christopher's correspondence studies until they could find a secondary-level teacher.

Seasick or not, she too was glad to be back on a ship. No matter how long they lived on land she just couldn't seem to adjust to most people's perception of the world. Even church friends had different priorities. But Dave and Joy acknowledged that others probably found them just as frustrating. For them, fulfilment lay in knowing they were 100 per cent engaged in advancing God's Kingdom. It was an extra blessing to discover that the motion of their new home did not cause Joy the severe seasickness she suffered on the old *Logos*.

Joy's duties added up to a full-time job, yet allowed flexibility for other activities. She and Dave became the 'parents' of one of the fellowship groups for single crew and staff members. Regular wives' meetings were also a chance for encouragement and problem-solving. The ship had a ministry to women in most ports and Joy sometimes participated in conferences, giving a testimony or sitting on a panel discussion. Often she served as a hostess at conferences and official opening receptions. Through the years, she and Dave were introduced to dozens of ambassadors and heads of state such as the President of Malta and King of Zululand.

The food facilities on *Logos II* were an improvement, allowing crew members to make occasional treats if they chose. Joy even had a microwave in their cabin. Learning how to bake with such an oven could be tricky, as a cake might come out looking undecidedly uneven if they were sailing in heavy seas. On Sundays, when the children were a bit older, the family enjoyed having suppers together in the cabin.

The *Logos II* sailed on her maiden voyage in 1990. Reaching Eastern Europe just after the historic lifting of the Iron Curtain was a thrill. So was sailing down the Neva River to St Petersburg, the first non-Soviet ship allowed to visit in over seventy years. Russian believers gave the crew an emotional welcome. Although book sales were not allowed, hundreds attended conferences and stood for hours in the book fair, hungrily reading. Staff members turned their backs when some of the books and Bibles disappeared. But the crew were allowed to blitz the city with gospel tracts and even held open-air programmes on the steps of the Museum of Atheism. Even the children were awed by a field trip to the famous Hermitage.

After Eastern Europe came the United Kingdom and then West Africa and South America. In 1992, Christopher turned sixteen and Joy took him back to England for high school qualification exams. He then stayed on for nearly two years with a church family, to complete pre-university exams. The rest of the family returned to Britain a year later. They had reached a crossroads. Operation Mobilization's leadership wanted them to spend some time off the ship after so long on board; however, Heather's schooling meant they couldn't go to the ships office in Germany. The UK leader suggested they could stand in for him while he took a sabbatical. But when he was instead appointed co-ordinator for Western Europe, Dave was formally requested to replace him as OM's UK field leader.

Dave was very hesitant to accept the position, aware that it didn't fit his gifting. The following years in Oswestry, near the Welsh border, were certainly a challenge. On the positive side they both appreciated the chance to grasp an overview of the work, rather than just the ships. It was also a nice change to work more 'sensible' hours and live in a spacious home.

Chris was able to visit them while attending university and Heather was occupied with school activities. Joy was content enough to work full time in the finance department. But they did miss the ship. And after five years as UK Director, Dave knew he would have to go to sea to renew his chief's ticket or re-sit the exam. A combination of circumstances eventually led him to give up his responsibilities so that he could fill in for stretches on the *Logos II*. When Heather finished her pre-university exams in 2000 and went for a year to the *MV Doulos*, Dave and Joy both moved back on the *Logos II*.

It was strange to be back on the ship after the long seven-year gap, especially without the children. Only one person remained on board who still knew them, and it was harder to make friends. Yet slipping back into the rhythm of ship life wasn't difficult. After several months in Turkey the *Logos II* sailed to Beirut, where over 85,000 queued up to visit. Later they went on to Spain and other parts of Europe. Joy enjoyed working in the book fair, and handling travel arrangements for people who were leaving the ship. Giving younger recruits advice and encouraging other wives was also part of her work.

When a first engineer was needed on the *Doulos* in April 2001, Dave and Joy volunteered to fly out to

Singapore. This was their first time on the *Doulos* and it was a big adjustment. With a complement of over 300 people compared to the 200 on *Logos II*, the ship was a lot larger. Even many of the long-term staff on board didn't know them. In a way it was like starting all over again. While Dave worked in the engine room, Joy took care of the post and office supplies for the general office.

As postmistress she recalls when the mail arrived on a Christmas Eve, and she had to miss the Christmas programme in order to distribute the eagerly awaited parcels and letters. After a year, Joy moved to the crew library and transferred hundreds of cassette messages to computer format, giving them greater accessibility. Fortunately the larger ship was even steadier than the *Logos II*, although she still needed seasick tablets or sea-bands.

Joy and Dave covered thousands of nautical miles around Asia and Africa during their twenty months aboard the ship. Then they made another move. In February 2003 Dave agreed to take over as Technical Manager in the ship's office in Germany. The job, which involves finding the right equipment and supplies for the two vessels, re-ordering parts and arranging the *Doulos* dry dock, sometimes means being away from Joy for extended periods.

Germany has presented Joy with a totally new culture, language and lifestyle to get accustomed to. However, she is determined to surmount the challenges and tackle language-learning. She also helps out in the ship's finance department. Dave's assignment will probably last until another ship replaces the *Logos II*. But with God's enabling, Dave and Joy expect to spend a few more years at sea before retirement. Their enthusiasm for the ministry does not diminish. It is a privilege to be part of carrying the message of the gospel, good books and practical aid where they are most needed.

'We have been blessed to see the effect of the ships on thousands of visitors, from government ministers to street children,' recalls Joy. 'We have also witnessed the power of God working in the young people who serve as staff, receiving training and exposure to the world they can't get anywhere else.'

Dave and Joy have loved to find ex-ship people wherever they go, continuing to build Christ's Kingdom as church leaders or career missionaries.

In spite of the fact that seasickness has always been her 'thorn in the flesh', Joy has learned to accept her weakness and even work around it.

'I believe that God allows such things to slow his servants down, and remind them he's the one our busyness is all about,' she comments. 'Being flat on your back,' she says, 'forces you to rearrange priorities.'

Sometimes Joy thinks about what life might have been like had they gone to Bangladesh. The chances are she would have had more of a chance to develop a ministry of her own. At sea, Dave has the priority role; her responsibility is support and maintenance. But neither of them doubts that in the Lord's eyes, everyone is equally significant.

And as long as he remains their captain at the helm neither illness or shipwreck, the loss of a child or even the end of life itself can keep his loved ones from reaching the port of heaven.

VITAL STATISTICS: Domestic violence

Domestic violence is the most widespread form of abuse against women in the world today. Between one-quarter and one-half of women have been abused by a partner. Only 44 countries specifically protect women against domestic violence.[1]

- Battering is the single largest cause of injury to women aged between fifteen and forty-four in the **United States**: more than mugging, car accidents and rape combined.
- A recent BBC report revealed that in the UK two women a week are killed by current or former partners.[2] Women married to Muslim men are eight times more likely to be killed by their spouses than any other women in **Britain**.

LATIN AMERICA

Courts in many countries are reluctant to rule on domestic violence, considering it a family matter. A judge in Chile found that violence within the home was not a crime and did not fall within the court's jurisdiction.

In Mexico, only eleven out of thirty-two states have changed their seventeenth-century civil and penal codes to make domestic violence a crime. In the remaining states, beating wives or children is not considered an offence.

The Colombian Institute of Family Welfare has estimated that 95 per cent of abuse cases in the country are not reported.[3]

JAPAN

Domestic violence has been pervasive in Japan for so long that it is considered a normal part of marriage. Abuse was only talked about publicly in 1998. A national survey conducted in February 2000 by the Prime Minister's Office found that 1 out of 20 women are 'subjected to life-threatening violence'.[4] Many of the victims are housewives who are unable or unwilling to seek assistance. Japan offers only about 40 shelters for battered women.

Wives murdered by their husbands constitute approximately 30 per cent of all the murders committed in the country. In the year 2000, cases of injury resulting in death, in which a 'husband kills his wife as a result of continuous hitting and kicking', received a sentence of only six to eight years imprisonment.[5] A new law enacted in 2001 is designed to help protect victims, but enforcement is difficult since only 1–10 per cent of women report abuse.

- Women in **Swaziland** are expected to remain silent when they are abused. In fact, the Swati word for 'wife' or 'woman' means 'one who dies without speaking of what she has endured'. Swaziland has only recently begun drafting laws against sexual offences, and prosecuting rape cases.
- A 2003 Human Rights Watch report, 'Just Die Quietly: Domestic Violence and Women's Vulnerability to HIV in Uganda' documents widespread rape and brutal attacks on women by their husbands in **Uganda**, where a specific domestic violence law has not been enacted and where spousal rape is not criminalized.
- In **India** a kidnapping or abduction happens every 4 minutes, a dowry death every 10 minutes, a rape every 54 minutes, an act of cruelty every 33 minutes and a criminal offence against women every 7 minutes.[6]
- Hundreds of women in **Bangladesh** have had acid thrown in their faces by men who say they have dishonoured them in some way, such as rejecting a

marriage proposal. Even children have been scarred. A man may get revenge on an enemy by burning the faces of his wife and daughters. The crime is most common in Bangladesh and Afghanistan, but also happens in Pakistan. Women are increasingly being attacked by husbands for minor offences, such as not having dinner ready or refusing sex. The man is very seldom prosecuted.[7]

PAKISTAN

In 1979 Pakistan's rape laws changed. In the new 'Offence of Zina Ordinance', statutory rape, previously defined as sex with or without the consent of a girl under the age of fourteen, was no longer a crime. In addition, the legal possibility of marital rape was eliminated.

Although some victims may have no chance of fending off an attacker, judges seem to require that they resist to the point of suffering visible physical injury if they wish to see their attackers punished. In 1997, for instance, a Federal Shariat Court converted a rape conviction to one of fornication on the grounds that '[since] no violence was found on her body, it could be reasonable to infer that she was a willing party to sexual intercourse'.

In addition, an attacker will never receive the maximum penalty unless the victim comes up with 'four adult, pious, male Muslim witnesses'. The victim's testimony alone is not enough, nor would four female witnesses be acceptable.

The great majority of police, doctors and prosecutors in Pakistan not only disbelieve but also belittle women who report a rape. Police have even been known to threaten and intimidate victims and accept bribes from accused males.

One attorney openly declared, 'I don't believe in rape cases. Women's consent is always there. If rape exists, it happens in only 1 per cent of cases.' In fact, the woman who files an accusation is herself in danger of prosecution, unless she can prove that she was not a willing partner in adultery or fornication. In other words, the victim herself is guilty until proven innocent. Human rights workers say that approximately half the women who report a rape are charged with adultery without any substantiating evidence. Pakistani jails are full of them. Even when acquitted such women may fall victim to 'honour killings' by male members of their family, who consider their honour compromised. In traditional villages, girls or women who bear an illegitimate child after being molested may be stoned to death.

Pakistan has no specific laws for domestic violence. Abuse in the home is most likely to be dismissed as a family matter. In the rare case that it does go to a criminal court, a monetary settlement (blood money) or retribution may be awarded.

Notes

1 United Nations High Commission for Refugees (UNHCR), 2003.
2 Sue Littlemore, BBC News Online, 18th February 2004.
3 US Department of State, 'Colombia Country Report on Human Rights', 2002, p. 57.
4 Ikeuchi, Hiromi, 'Japanese Women Now', Women's Online Media.
5 Nobuhiro Suzuki, 'Socio-Cultural Background of Domestic Violence in Japan', Project Blue Sky, National Commission for Women Report, *Asian Age*, 9th March 2000.
6 Nobuhiro Suzuki, 'Socio-Cultural Background of Domestic Violence in Japan', 9th March 2000.
7 Shia News, 'Acid Attacks: The Agony of Pakistani Women', 9th June 2003. Cited on {http://www.angelifire.com/journal/achingheart/women/acid.html}

VITAL STATISTICS: Education

Two-thirds of the world's 880 million illiterates are
women. Of the 300 million children without access to
education, 200 million are girls. The number of
illiterates is not expected to decrease significantly in
the next 20 years.

● While school enrolment has increased for children in most
countries, the gender gap still persists. In most low-
income countries, parents are more likely to send their
sons to school. If they do attend, girls are often obliged to
drop out early. Less than one-fourth of girls in developing
countries attend secondary school.

PERCENTAGE OF STUDENTS ATTENDING SECONDARY SCHOOL THAT ARE GIRLS, BASED ON A FIVE-YEAR STUDY BETWEEN 1992 AND 1997

Country	Percentage of female students (%)
Yemen	20
Iraq	38
India	39
Turkey	39
Netherlands	47
Korea	48
USA	49
Spain	51

Source: United Nations, *The World's Women, Trends and
Statistics* (New York, updated 2002).

- In Southern Asia, nearly three out of five women cannot read or write. A third of Indian girls do not finish primary school. An estimated half of all women in Africa and in the Arab region are still illiterate.
- In **Saudi Arabia**, schooling for girls has never been compulsory. Mixed schooling is forbidden. The country didn't get its first school for girls until 1956. The female literacy rate in 1970 was the lowest in the Middle East, only 2 per cent. In 1980, 23 per cent of girls were enrolled in a secondary school. But today female literacy is up to 50 per cent. Given the chance, female students have proven themselves. Women's university test scores in Saudi Arabia routinely outstrip men's.

TEN WORST ILLITERACY RATES AMONG WOMEN OVER THE AGE OF TWENTY-FIVE

Country	Illiteracy rate (%)
Mauritania	83
Ivory Coast	85
Central African Republic	87
Djibouti	87
Benin	88
Senegal	88
Nepal	89
Mali	91
Yemen	92

Source: United Nations, *The World's Women, Trends and Statistics* (New York, updated 2002).

EDUCATION AND INFANT MORTALITY

- Studies show that one of the main factors influencing mortality rates of children under the age of five is the mother's education level. A 10 per cent increase in female literacy reduced child mortality by 10 per cent in thirteen African countries between 1975 and 1985.
- A recent study into 63 countries showed that an improvement in women's education was 'the single largest contributor' to declines in malnutrition among children.

Nearly a billion people entered the twenty-first century unable to read a book, or sign their own names.

Chapter 4

Little house on the frontier

'Anything I've ever done that ultimately was worthwhile . . .
initially scared me to death.'

Betty Bender

An all-American tomboy, Pam Olson was happiest when she was astride a horse, hunting or fishing. She took a keen interest in riding competitions and took away her share of ribbons. Her hard-working family was part of a small Wisconsin farming community of six hundred, where church going was expected. But the preaching didn't penetrate very deeply as far as Pam was concerned. She found her teenage kicks in dates, drugs and drinking.

It was while she was joyriding around town with friends that the police stopped the car she was in, and discovered marijuana in the trunk. The seventeen-year-old was shaken. She had no idea that it was there. And although the charges against her were eventually dropped, the incident drove her to the Bible for the first time. For some reason Pam kept on reading, compelled by a hunger she didn't understand. Much later she was to learn she had been the special focus of her aunt and uncle's prayers.

By January 1977 Pam knew she had found what she was looking for. She gave her life over to Jesus Christ. The results were so dramatic that at least one of her teachers suspected she was high on drugs. After moving to a parish in another town, her pastor's wife helped her enrol in a correspondence Bible study. But nobody had to urge Pam to share her faith. Nothing could quench her enthusiastic witness for Christ. The fourth year that she competed in her school's track and field events, she ran for the Lord as much as for her parents. Her coaches voted her the most valued – and most improved – player.

Following high school Pam attended a six-week 'Agape Force' training camp for discipling young believers. Along with others she surrendered the total Lordship of her life to Jesus. Then she put words into action by making restitution to all the people she had wronged in the past. That winter she used all of her farm earnings to attend another course run by Youth With A Mission (YWAM), in Hawaii. Pam's eyes were opened wide to the possibility of serving God in other countries. Enrolling in Bethany College of Missions in Minnesota seemed the next logical step.

The next four years at Bethany completed the metamorphosis of the former rebel-without-a-cause. Although Pam didn't know it, the Lord was putting her into training for the years ahead, stretching her mentally and spiritually in all directions. Her stubborn will finally yielded to his. She agreed to go wherever he wanted to send her.

Mercifully, God's plan for Pam included a partner. Dave was a fellow Bethany student who not only shared Pam's love and gratitude to God but also had the same energetic commitment to serve him. Pam and Dave Lovett united their lives in marriage after finishing their studies. When snow fell on their honeymoon camping trip, the pair laughingly agreed it was good missionary training.

In 1983 the couple set off for India with Operation Mobilization. Three years later they moved to spend another few years in Bangladesh. The birth of their first child, Rachel, forced Pam to learn how to juggle mother-hood with ministry. She was just making headway on speaking Bengali when they moved again, finishing off their sub-continent experience with eighteen months in Pakistan. This time they focused on refugees on the Afghanistan border, spending much of their time learning to speak passable Dari.

Seeing God change lives on the frontier of a Muslim country was deeply fulfilling. But in the autumn of 1989 the ex-patriot Christian community was rocked by the kidnapping of Canadian John Tarzwell. No trace of the husband and father of three was ever found, and he was eventually pronounced dead, the victim of Muslim extremists.

The loss of their co-worker was a sharp blow to Pam and Dave. They had both been deeply shocked a few years earlier at the brutal murder of Bethany classmates, serving God in a Muslim area of the Philippines. Now they realized they had been among the last people to talk to John. Pam still shudders at the memory of a day shortly after the kidnapping, when Dave found himself being watched by a Pushtun man in their neighbour-hood. The man caught his eye and drew his hand across his throat, with a meaningful leer. Pam, already suffering ill effects from her second pregnancy, was unable to shake off her foreboding.

Deteriorating health finally forced Pam and Dave to return to the United States. Their son Justin was born in May 1990, and Dave used the next year to study for a Masters degree in Cross-cultural Education and Missions at Wheaton College. Pam was also able to audit some classes. Their plan was to go back to Pakistan after Dave's graduation. But sometime during that year his attention was captivated by an even more critical need. Tajikistan had just managed to achieve independence from Russia, but the beautiful, mountainous Central Asian nation was paying for its freedom with a disastrous civil war. It was now one of the poorest places on earth. Eighty per cent of its people lived below the poverty line, with an average family scraping by on only about seventeen dollars a month.

The compass of Dave's heart began to swing towards Tajikistan. Pam, however, dug in her heels.

'We have already set up homes in three other countries, and studied two new languages,' she argued. Their ministry among Afghan refugees in Pakistan was bearing fruit. Why should their little family start all over again in a country that was far from safe?

But the sense that God wanted them to take his love to the forgotten Tajiks didn't go away. Both Pam and Dave were pioneer types, and no one else seemed prepared to take on such a mammoth challenge.

So Pam put out a fleece. She prayed that if God truly wanted them to go, he would somehow supply the 25,000 dollars they would need for moving and resettling. To her complete astonishment a young woman who was unaware of Pam's prayer came forward at a Sunday morning service that same week to offer the exact sum. Pam could no longer argue. In January 1992 she wrote in her cloth-bound diary: 'Lord God, I am afraid . . . Keep us safe in Tajikistan.' That autumn the Central Asia Development Agency (CADA) was officially registered. The family flew out to the capital city of Dushanbe in January 1993.

Pam vividly recalls the day they arrived with thirty-five bags, a six-year-old toddler, and no place to live.

Persistent bladder trouble had added to her misery during the trip.

'The nightmare of changing planes in Moscow was the last straw and reduced me to tears. Finally, after landing in Dushanbe and driving to the house Dave had rented for us, we discovered it had been taken over by refugees!'

Mercifully, God led them to another and better place, almost at once. By the end of the first day they were sleeping in their new home.

The country was still reeling from the deaths of tens of thousands of men and boys in a civil war that was to continue until 1997. Thirty thousand women would emerge from this war as widows. A fifth of residents would see their homes destroyed. With continuing sporadic violence between rival leaders, the Lovetts lived under a curfew that continued through their first few years. The real danger of the situation was brought home when they attended funerals of some Russian Christians who had been shot, most probably by the mafia. Pam's nerves were stretched to near breaking whenever Dave had to travel away from home. A few times she even heard would-be intruders on the roof, but God was faithful. Their house was never broken into while Dave was away.

Tajikistan's devastated infrastructure meant that even basic foods like milk, eggs, sugar and flour were often unobtainable. Items they found in the bazaars one day disappeared the next. Unhygienic conditions dictated that all vegetables and fruits should be soaked in iodine and drinking water was both boiled and filtered. In the bathtub, tap water trickled out in a coffee-coloured stream. The family pondered the benefit of bathing, when they couldn't even see their legs in the water.

Telephones varied, working from 10 per cent to 25 per cent of the time. Gas and electricity were also in short supply. Fortunately, the Lovetts had a wood stove to fall back on for winter heat when all else failed. Some of the first staff to join CADA were obliged to cook their meals outdoors on kerosene heaters. The family had experienced tough living conditions before in India, Bangladesh and Pakistan. But Tajikistan topped them all.

The absence of an adequate health system was, perhaps, most worrying. Doctors and hospitals just didn't have the medicines and equipment necessary to fight disease. Patients were sometimes turned away, hospitals shutting down for weeks at a time during epidemics. Killer diseases like meningitis, typhoid, tuberculosis and respiratory illnesses claimed countless men, women and children.

The Lovetts lost no time setting up an office in their home and plunging headlong into the sea of destitution. Their priority had to be finding, importing and distributing tons of food, medical supplies and clothing. Without exaggeration, their efforts were to prove a matter of life over death for thousands. Local residents still talk about CADA's arrival when no one else seemed to care. The agency's stated goal was 'to relieve suffering and improve the lives of the people of Central Asia, both physically and spiritually'. The government knew they were Christians and the KGB kept tabs on them. But although working through the bureaucracy felt like 'swimming in molasses', nobody hindered their life-saving efforts.

Pam was impatient with the recurring bladder trouble that robbed her of the energy she so much needed to set up their new home. At the end of the first month she expressed her discouragement in her diary: 'I don't see myself cut out for doing this pioneer work in Tajikistan . . . Lord, to get better here is almost impossible unless you intervene for me. Please help me to sleep the whole night through.' A few days later she noted, 'I think I heard tanks last night go by our house . . . Lord, I can't believe you have placed us in a war zone. Please keep us safe in the hollow of your hands.'

Pam's journals served as a release valve during the next ten years. Not only was Tajikistan a war zone but the tragic recipient of floods, droughts, famines, earthquakes, epidemics, bombs and kidnappings. As their work expanded, the Lovetts moved the office to another house and finally into a large building in downtown Dushanbe. National workers were employed. By popular demand an English Learning Centre was added to the relief work, then business training. Both of these courses helped local Tajiks find better jobs and qualify for study abroad. CADA created the country's first e-mail centre, which came to be heavily relied upon by Dushanbe's business and professional community. Health care and development projects multiplied as skilled staff members – both foreign and national – joined the team. Such practical measures not only helped to rebuild Tajikistan's infrastructure; it gave the staff credibility as Christians. The number of Tajik believers began slowly to grow. New fellowships were established.

Dave thrived on each new challenge. Sometimes it seemed to Pam that his devotion to the birth and growth of CADA came ahead of her and the children. And whenever her husband had to leave the country on business, problems at home invariably increased. Even normal household chores took twice as long on the frontier, given the shortages of clean water and power. And the absence of acceptable educational facilities forced Pam to home-school her children for the first four years. In addition to this, new team members always needed help to settle in, and crises in the lives of Tajik friends and neighbours could not be ignored. The Lovett home was the crossroads for almost non-stop traffic. But although keeping priorities straight wasn't easy, Pam was determined to make their home a haven for the family.

Their first Thanksgiving Day in November was a memorable one. At five o'clock in the morning a loud pounding at the gate of their compound awoke Pam and Dave.

'Please! Can you help me?' The man at their gate was obviously desperate. 'My wife – she's pregnant. She seems to have gone into premature labour!'

He asked to use their telephone to call an ambulance, and borrowed scissors and thread.

Soon after he came running back with an infant wrapped in his winter coat. An old Russian woman followed, leading the baby's mother who was still on her feet, and bleeding. Pam brought her into the house and got her to lie down until an ambulance arrived. A lady doctor delivered the placenta right in the Lovetts' living room and mother and baby were eventually conveyed to the hospital.

A few days following this incident, Pam received the shocking news of a fire that had destroyed much of her family home in Wisconsin. Although both of her parents escaped injury, the trauma caused her father to suffer a small heart attack. As if that wasn't enough, the ambulance transporting him to the hospital was involved in an accident. Fortunately he was again spared, but ended up having to undergo four-way bypass heart surgery.

She recalls, 'It was during times like these that I was torn in two, longing to be with family thousands of miles away, but knowing I couldn't leave my responsibilities on the frontier.'

'Tajikistan isn't the end of the world,' Dave sometimes told friends, 'but you can see it from here.'

Central Asia did not offer many outlets for releasing stress. There were no modern restaurants for a relaxing evening out. No bowling allies or tennis courts or swimming pools. Not even television in English, although they could watch videos they bought or that friends sent them. The family went for an occasional hike in the hills for outings together, and in later years they secured their own *dacha* or cottage to escape to, with its own fruit garden and place to swim. But Pam sorely missed her horses. She often contemplated getting one, but had to accept that riding wasn't culturally acceptable for women. Even walking alone in the city was hazardous. Girls and women were reported molested or dragged into cars and raped. Mafia violence flourished in an atmosphere of political instability.

Brief getaways to the United States or another country each year were essential for survival. Besides the chance to see doctors and dentists, and take care of ministry-connected business, they were precious times of catching up with friends and family members. Pam was pleased to be able to help her parents move into their refurbished home during their second visit back. On the farm the family rode, camped, fished, canoed and swam to their contentment. A few times they fitted in a trip to Disneyland. Another year their church provided a home away from home on a Wisconsin lake.

The Lovetts were on route to such a break in June 1994 when their travel documents went missing. Pam had been fully occupied with caring for her sick daughter on the flight to Moscow and hadn't been aware of the leather pouch slipping under her seat. It contained all of the essential items: passports, tickets for their onward journey to New York, even credit cards and money. In

Moscow they reported their loss to the airport authorities, praying (admittedly without much hope) that the pouch would somehow turn up. Then they raced around the city to apply for new passports, wire for more money from the States and make arrangements for a place to stay the night. They were just about to return to the airport to pay 800 dollars in fines for new visas when the impossible happened: tickets, wallet and passports were returned intact at the airport information desk. By nine o'clock that night they were free to resume their journey.

God stepped in to save the day on many occasions. But Satan never missed a chance, either. By the mid 1990s, other aid groups and non-government agencies had moved into Tajikistan. A few of them seconded staff members to work with CADA. When two families decided to leave their agency for what seemed like 'greener pastures' in another organization, it was deeply disappointing. Around the same time, Pam and another couple fell ill with hepatitis A. Then to top it all off, 1000 dollars were stolen from their safe.

The Lovetts' spirits sank to a low ebb. Even the city electricity seemed to conspire against them, leaving most of their house without power for days. Then someone at the office plugged in a computer without the transformer and it blew. Pam wrote: 'Dave is ready to quit. So am I . . . but it's another opportunity to trust God for his purposes to be worked out.'

CADA staff members soldiered on, helping the Tajik people rebuild their nation. Twenty-five thousand Russian troops were billeted in the country as peacekeepers until 1997, when the civil war officially ended, but there were still occasional bursts of violence. That spring Dushanbe's infected water system caused a typhoid epidemic. Fifty thousand cases were reported in and around the city.

Pam longed to be able to initiate other ministries for the poor and oppressed living all around her. Ideas ran from rescuing girls from sexual abuse to feeding beggar children and sharing Jesus with them. She even contemplated ways to reach the black market dollar-changers and mafia. But the daily demands of caring for her family, home schooling and housework used up most of her time. There were also ever-erupting minor crises, like their pet dog getting distemper and having to be put down or the children catching head lice, probably from friends, necessitating a top-to-bottom housecleaning, spraying and de-lousing of bedding and clothing. In 1999 a not-so-minor fire broke out in the wall and roof of their home. About six months later another blaze damaged their translation office and the studio where worship songs were being recorded in Tajik.

Ill health also continued to stalk Pam. Along with the stomach bugs epidemic in that part of the world she went through bouts of dysentery and urinary tract infections, skin allergies and bronchitis, hepatitis, gall stones, pneumonia and even food poisoning. An added weight was the anxiety attacks and spells of depression caused by a chemical imbalance in her system. Finding the right treatment in Tajikistan wasn't easy. In a diary entry in May 1998 she cried, 'I am so worn out. Last night I really blew it in front of the kids. I am such a bad example. How can God use me?'

Again and again, he showed her that his strength was made perfect in weakness. Pam managed to make time for weekly Bible studies with Tajik women friends. Seeing a number of them come to faith and take their first steps with Christ was one of her greatest joys. One year the team held a Christmas programme for a hundred women, and several of them became Christians. As the church grew, so did the need for Tajik children's Bibles, gospels and other basic literature. Once a teacher was found to take over the education of expatriate children, Pam was free to get involved in translation projects. Soon she was overseeing a team of seven Tajik translators and editors. She also duplicated Christian videos. Sometimes Rachel helped her copy hundreds of videos into Tajik, Russian, Uzbek and English languages, for distribution throughout the country.

In 1999 CADA was officially brought under the larger relief and development agency, Operation Mercy. Dave also turned over the field's team leadership so that he could concentrate fully on CADA's work. The possibility arose of moving to another country.

Pam struggled to accept this new role. The OM team in Tajikistan was, after all, their 'baby'. They had nursed the field through all its growing pains. It was hard to see a co-worker take over its leadership. 'It still brings tears to my eyes to let it go,' she confided in her diary. 'I believe it is a grieving process I will have to go through. Like letting a child go. . .' Then she added, 'During prayer time tonight it was precious how the Spirit moved on us to pray for each other.'

Only the previous summer, during a break in the States, Pam had found herself reflecting how 'Tajik' the family had become in their thinking and behaviour. Rachel and Justin were truly 'third-culture' kids, neither fully Tajik nor fully American. They had experienced their share of tough times in Dushanbe, but they had also received great benefits from their unorthodox upbringing. And both were firmly in love with the Lord.

Fortunately, the Lovetts did not have to pull up stakes in Tajikistan after all. A prolonged drought created the worst famine in decades, and Dave's contacts and experience in the area were urgently required. Besides widespread crop failure, anthrax was infecting the cattle.

Neighbouring Afghanistan was also suffering from a rainless three years. More and more refugees poured over Tajikistan's border, fleeing both the repressive Taliban regime and starvation.

Tajikistan's own political situation was still far from stable. In the summer of 2001, serious fighting broke out again between rival factions. The Lovetts sometimes heard guns blasting away at the rebels only ten miles from their house. Bombs went off in various parts of the city and the mayor himself was badly injured.

At the same time, religious tension was spiralling. Most of Central Asia was rooted in Islam, although Communist Russia's long control of the area had left few residents with any deep faith. But a leaked letter written by the head of Tajikistan's religious affairs agency spoke of concern about the 'increased activity' of Christian churches. Local fellow-ships began to experience harassment and threats by KGB and Islamic groups. On a Sunday morning in October 2000 fundamentalists singled out a church and bombed it during a service. Ten worshippers died, and another 100 were wounded. Dave and Pam helped mobilize the distribution of tons of food, blankets and warm clothing to the destitute church members who remained.

The next year another Christian agency in Dushanbe was closed down, its workers ordered to leave the country. A CADA team member's wife demolished her car in a major road accident, although she herself escaped injury. Most tragically, the three-year-old son of other staff members had to be air-ambulanced out of the country when a pot of boiling soup fell on him. Fifty per cent of little Levi's body sustained third-degree burns. Five months later, he died.

Early one morning during the first week of September 2001, when the team was spending time in fasting and prayer, Pam woke abruptly from a frightening dream.

She told Dave that she felt something terrible was going to happen. She had seen themselves and their co-workers standing on top of a very tall building. In her dream an airplane had flown by. As it circled the building a wing crashed into it, cutting off the top, which fell into water at the bottom. All their fellow workers were unhurt.

Dave tried to reassure her. There were no tall buildings in Tajikistan. For skyscrapers she would have to go to New York City. A few days later they stared in horrified dismay as New York's World Trade Center crumbled to dust on their television screen. Most Tajiks condemned the terrorist attack on America. Their country soon came into new prominence as a strategic base for boosting the Northern Alliance's fight against the Taliban. Meanwhile, thousands of destitute Afghans were stranded at the borders without food, clothing and shelter. As one of the few relief agencies on the spot, CADA/Operation Mercy moved quickly to save lives.

By trucking aid across the hazardous terrain they managed to maintain a crucial lifeline to thousands of Afghan families. Some camped in freezing temperatures throughout that long winter. The next spring, when world attention was already receding, a severe earthquake in the north brought further devastation. Dave pleaded for emergency medical workers and supplies to supplement their already stretched resources. Through this effort the team were able to provide relief aid to over 500,000 Afghans, and projects were opened in other key cities.

The summer of 2002 marked nearly ten years since the Lovetts had first arrived in Tajikistan. In spite of the ongoing crisis, the family decided to go ahead with plans to take twelve months' home assignment in the States. Pam's uterus was diseased and she would require a partial hysterectomy. Rachel and Justin deserved the chance to rediscover their national roots. And the family were eager to renew contacts with friends and family, churches and supporters. Of course, even with an acting director in place, Dave would continue overseeing the work in Tajikistan and Afghanistan.

God alone could decide how long the Lovetts would continue to make their home in Central Asia. Rachel had now reached sixteen, and to insure an adequate level of education she would need to go to a Christian boarding school. Dave's new role as Regional Director of Operation Mercy was likely to take him away from home more than ever. As for Pam – well, Pam was only sure of one thing. The adventure was not yet over. Nor would it end as long as the Lord chose to use them – wherever it was – to touch lives for eternity.

VITAL STATISTICS: Female infanticide

The killing of female children, before and after birth, has been called 'the biggest single holocaust in human history'.[1]

The death toll from 'gendercide' throughout the centuries would amount to mega-millions. The practice of murdering baby girls in preference to boys goes back to the days of ancient Rome.

INDIA

- Two million babies are aborted in India every year, the vast majority of them female.
- The birth of a girl to poor Indian families often causes dismay. A daughter must eventually be married off, and marriage dowries require such an enormous expenditure that it can bankrupt the family.[2] Many parents therefore want a girl's life to end before it even begins. The development of prenatal sex determination tests in the 1970s led to wide scale sex-selective abortions. Even upper-caste families can regard girls as an economic burden and see foeticide as an option. Ultrasound scanning is now illegal, but few if any doctors have been prosecuted and sex determination and abortion clinics are commonplace. Their advertisements urge the investment of a few hundred rupees (7 dollars) on a gender test in order to save thousands on a future dowry.
- Those who cannot afford pre-natal tests must wait until they give birth to their babies. Newborn females may then be smothered, strangled or simply allowed to starve to death. Some infants have been fed salt, milk laced with poison or dry unhulled rice that punctured their windpipes.
- In some villages in Rajasthan, northern India, the birth of daughters has not been allowed for years. The resulting unbalanced sex ratio has forced the Gurjjar tribe men to share a wife in the family.[3]

- Only two mothers in recent years have received life imprisonment sentences for infanticide; a few others are serving six months to three years. However, the woman is usually given no choice: the decision lies with the woman's husband or in-laws. She must obey or suffer herself.[4]
- India's 2001 census showed it had the lowest female to male ratio in the world: 927 females born to 1000 males. Five states had under 880 females to 1000 males. The statistical norm is 1050 females for every 1000 males. India's government report of October 2003, entitled 'Missing: Mapping the Adverse Child Sex Ratio in India', confirms that more infanticides and foeticides are taking place now than a decade ago.[5]

CHINA

The World Health Organization estimates more than 50 million women have gone 'missing' in China, because of the institutionalized killing and neglect of girls.

- Infanticide of girl babies in China goes back far before pre-People's Republic days. Daughters have been called 'maggots in the rice' because they take food that could go to nourish boys. In the Chinese culture, the male can earn more and it is the son who looks after the parents in old age. Although female infanticide largely disappeared during from the 1950s to 1970s, it surged back in the 1980s after the imposing of a 'one child' policy. The government has now outlawed the use of ultrasound for sex determination, but many doctors still use it.
- A national census released in 2002 showed an imbalance of more than 116 male births recorded for every 100 female births. Officials in Beijing fear this will damage the country's future social and economic stability, and further encourage the trade in kidnapped women.[6]

> Until the turn of the century, daughters were often given no name at all. Today those born in rural areas may still be given the names 'Alidi', 'Zhaodi' or 'Yindi', meaning *'bring a little brother'*.

Notes

1 Joseph Farah, 'Cover-up of China's gender-cide', Western Journalism Center/FreeRepublic, 29th September 1997.
2 Dowries can amount to several times more than the head of the house many earn in a year.
3 *India Today*, 3rd September 2003.
4 Sampath Kumar, 'India Rights Campaign for Infanticide Mothers', BBC News Online, 17th July 2003.
5 This report was published as a joint effort between the Registrar-General of India, the Department of Family Welfare and the United Nations Population Fund.
6 John Gittings, 'Growing Sex Imbalance Shocks China', *The Guardian*, 13th May 2002.

VITAL STATISTICS: Female circumcision

An estimated 130 million girls and women worldwide
have suffered female circumcision, even in the West.
Six thousand girls per day are at risk.

WHAT IS 'FEMALE CIRCUMCISION'?

Female circumcision, more accurately called female genital
mutilation (FGM) refers to the removal of part or all of the
female genitalia. There are three types. The most severe
practice is **infibulation**, carried out upon an estimated 15
per cent of girls that undergo FGM. The procedure involves
removing all or part of the clitoris (clitoridectomy), excision
(removing all or part of the *labia minora*), and the cutting of
the *labia majora* to create raw surfaces.[1] The vast majority of
FGM in Africa consists of clitoridectomy or excision. This is
also practised in the Middle East: Egypt, Oman, Yemen and
the United Arab Emirates. In Djibouti, an estimated 95 per
cent of women are infibulated.

Circumcision may be carried out any time from a girl's birth
to her first pregnancy. Sometimes it is regarded as a coming-of-
age ritual. But the most common age is between four and eight
years old. The person who performs it can be an older woman
or barber, a midwife or traditional healer or a qualified doctor.

Only the wealthy have access to doctors and anaesthetics.
The vast majority of girls are given no preparation or
painkiller. They are simply held down while the appointed
'surgeon' proceeds with a broken glass, tin lid, scissors,
razor blade or other cutting instrument. Antiseptic powder
may be applied, or more usually pastes containing herbs,
milk, eggs, ashes or dung which are believed to facilitate
healing. The girl may be taken to a specially designated
place to recover where, if the mutilation has been carried out
as part of an initiation ceremony, she receives traditional
teaching.

Why FGM?

In most societies where female circumcision is practiced, it is a deeply rooted tradition. A girl is not accepted into womanhood, and certainly not marriage, without this ritual. She is treated as unclean. Parents also regard FGM as a way to protect the chastity of daughters by reducing their sexual desire (although many mistakenly believe it actually increases fertility). Infibulation, in particular, is seen to safeguard the family honour.

- Even though no Qur'anic text mandates the practice, one in five Muslim girls today live in a community that sanctions some form of FGM. Few religious leaders have spoken up against it.
- In some African countries, more than half of all women and girls have undergone female circumcision. These numbers are not decreasing.

> 'How can we leave our daughters uncircumcised?' asked the mayor of an Egyptian city. 'The government can do what it wants and we, too, will do what we want. We will all circumcise our daughters, no matter what the punishments.'
> Osman Antar, Mayor of Sabee, Egypt, quoted in news report, 6th January 1998.[2]

> A forty-three-year-old female biology professor from the Sudan explained: 'We are brought up to believe that all sorts of evil things will happen to us if we are not circumcised. It is done at such a young age . . . It doesn't really sink in, what has been done, and the problems later when you are a woman, seem to have no connection to it.'
> From an interview with Eclas, a forty-three-year-old Sudanese biology professor.[3]

CONSEQUENCES

Girls undergoing FGM experience psychological trauma, pain and shock. Haemorrhage and tissue damage can cause death. In the days that follow, serious infections and abscesses often develop. Infibulation may also lead to long-term urinary tract infections, kidney damage, stones, infection from obstructing the menstrual flow, and even infertility.

A possible additional danger from all types of FGM is that repeated use of the same instrument on several girls, as is sometimes the case, can cause the spread of HIV. Lasting damage to the genital area can also increase the risk of HIV transmission during intercourse.

Many women report that on their wedding nights their husbands had to use a knife to cut a wider opening for intercourse. As one can imagine, impromptu surgery like this can cause even further damage to young brides.

During childbirth, scar tissue left from FGM may tear. Women who have been infibulated must be cut to allow delivery. After each birth the opening is re-stitched.[4]

Notes

1 *Labia minora* refers to the inner folds of skin surrounding the vagina; *labia majora* refers to the outer.
2 Osman Antar, 'Egyptian fundamentalists ignoring female circumcision ban', 6th January 1998, Agence France-Presse.
3 Hanny Lightfoot-Klein, *Prisoners of Ritual: Odyssey into Female Genital Circumcision in Africa*, (Binghamton, New York: Harrington Park Press, 1989) p. 116.
4 Female Genital Mutilation: A Human Rights Information Pack, Amnesty International. See: {http://www.amnesty.org/ailib/intcam/femgen/fgm1.htm}.

Chapter 5

Full circle

'To eat bread without hope is still slowly to starve to death.'
Pearl S. Buck

Almost everyone has heard of the killing fields of Communist Vietnam. To most they are only history. But for Cindy Lee and her family the reality of that terror will never completely fade. Nor will any of them forget the decision they took in 1978, to risk everything to escape.

The Lees had laid down their plans very carefully. Knowing they would increase their chances of survival if they split up, eighteen-year-old Cindy was paired off with one of her five brothers. These two were chosen to make the first attempt at leaving the country. Their escape route, however, turned out to be a trap. The pair were arrested. Not until they had suffered a month in prison did the rest of the family learn what happened. They managed to buy their release with a bribe.

The next time, Cindy's uncle arranged the escape. Along with her uncle's family, her mother and one of her four sisters, Cindy crammed into a thirty-two-foot boat with seven hundred other desperate refugees. Most of the men lay packed in rows side by side, like sardines.

The vessel was weighted so far below the safety line that some would-be passengers changed their minds. These individuals, however, were beaten and forced back into the boat. The local official in charge had already taken their money and didn't want to risk discovery.

Under cover of night, the boat slipped silently away on the South China Sea. The men, women and children on board clasped their few possessions to them, terror intermingled with hope. They had no idea where they were going. Their vessel was simply following the currents south. The broiling sun rose overhead and the hours passed slowly. Then, as they drifted out of Vietnamese waters, they saw the sails of another large boat on the horizon. The refugees watched it approach with rising excitement. Surely this meant rescue and help. But their happiness turned to sick horror as they identified the flag flying from the vessel's mast: a skull and crossbones. Pirates! They were about to be boarded by one of the notorious gangs that roamed these waters in search of spoil. The refugees screamed as the brigands drew alongside, threw their anchor into the other boat and quickly jumped in themselves, brandishing guns.

Cindy knew they could expect no mercy. Most of their provisions and whatever possessions they had would be stolen. As for the girls and women, she shuddered. She had heard plenty of tales about these men, never believing that she would one day be coming face to face with them. But then the pirates began separating the men and women into different boats. If she was going to do anything, she'd better move fast. Cindy ducked through the noise and general confusion into the covered area of the boat used for cooking. Swiftly she smeared black grease from a pot onto her face. Then, catching sight of a filthy, ragged jacket she pulled that on, frantically hoping that she looked as repellant as she now smelled. But what could she do about her jade necklace? And her ring? They were her only two possessions of value and her insurance for the future. She thrust the ring into her mouth and tried to swallow it. It refused to go down, so with only seconds to spare she wound the necklace around the ring and shoved them both into her hair.

Would the pirates discover her treasure? Cindy trembled as men paused to run their eyes over her. With a disgusted snort they moved away. Why bother her when they had their pick of more attractive females?

When the pirates had finally finished with them, the passengers were herded back into their boat and cast off again. Altogether they were to spend seven interminable days at sea, dizzy with hunger, thirst and sickness. Three more times they were boarded by pirates. Each time Cindy managed to protect herself. Once they threw a girl overboard. The other passengers fished her from the sea and dragged her back on board. There was too little food to go around. Cindy's stomach ached and her neck was covered with sores from salt water splashing on her. During that week, three babies were added to the boat's already overcrowded population.

At last they neared land. A fishing boat approached and its owner said he would show them where to go if they gave him gold. The refugees came up with a pair of gold earrings and the man instructed them to stay where they were. Shortly after he left, a huge Malaysian Navy ship appeared and the refugees cheered. This time they were sure to be taken to a refugee camp. Here they would be safe at least; housed and fed on dry land.

But it was not to be. With dismay the company found themselves being towed back out to sea. After several hours they were cut loose and told to keep going.

A day later they came in sight of a small island belonging to the Indonesian archipelago. This time, in desperation, they damaged their boat so that they couldn't be turned away again. Some of the people swam to shore; the old and very young went in canoes supplied by the locals. Cindy sold a precious piece of jade from her necklace to buy food.

Eventually the authorities transported the refugees to a camp on Kuku Island, where they were left to survive for the next year in very basic conditions. But worse than their situation was the extreme anxiety they suffered for their missing loved ones. Cindy had heard no news of the rest of her family for six months. Then her uncle managed to trade his reserve money for a broken radio. Every night thereafter they huddled over it, straining to listen to the special radio channel that beamed refugee news from Australia. Relatives who had made their way to other parts of the world also listened. Everyone was desperate for some word of separated family members.

Then one night, as the channel crackled almost continuously with interference and Cindy's uncle fiddled with the knobs, a message broke clearly through the static: 'This is number ten sister Amy Lee, selecting this song for my sister Cindy Lee. We are in a Malaysia refugee camp on the way to Canada!'

Remembering that moment, Cindy always cries. The names of hundreds of people were called on that radio program each night. She could so easily have missed her sister's words, but she didn't. Later, Cindy learned that her 'number one' sister – who was already safe in Canada – also 'happened' to hear the message on that station the same night. It was a miracle.

Cindy sold another piece of jade from her necklace. This time with the money she sent a telegram to her oldest sister, still in Vietnam, to let her know where she and her mother and sister were. This sister wrote to the rest of the family when they made it to British Colombia.

They in turn immediately petitioned the government for permission to sponsor the immigration of three more members of their family. The government refused, on the grounds they were not earning sufficient income. The family then approached the Chinese Association, who also turned them down. But a Christian school friend of Cindy's sister in Vancouver heard about the situation and shared it with her congregation. The members of the Kamloops Alliance Church decided to get involved.

Cindy and her mother and sister were informed that they had sponsors. The three were put on a plane and flown from Indonesia to Vancouver, stopping on the way at an army immigration centre in Montreal, Quebec. At this facility the women were told to remove their old clothing. After it was taken away they were hosed down. Like animals, Cindy thought, trembling with the cold and humiliation. It was another moment she was not likely to forget.

But the church in Vancouver gave a warm welcome to the newcomers. They provided a well-furnished accommodation and stocked the refrigerator with food. They even supplied an allowance to cover their immediate needs.

But Cindy was proud. She had lived through Buddhism, Communism, the brutality of prison and pirate attacks. She didn't want to be dependent on anyone in this new country. She found a job as a hotel chambermaid and started work immediately. But even earning her own support she felt empty, alienated from everyone else. Each day she passed a river on the way to the hotel. After a few months she began to stare at it in a new way. Suicide would be so easy, she thought; over so quickly. So much better than being lonely and unhappy and different from everyone else.

One day a church friend called. Students from Regina Bible School were in town, she told Cindy, and one of them spoke Cantonese. Cindy could speak very little English, so she and her sister Wendy went along to the program. They listened to the Chinese student share the words of John 3:16 and explain how God had loved everyone in the world enough to send his only Son. When he asked if the girls wanted to believe in Jesus, both of them were ready to say yes.

After a year in Kamloops, Cindy found a better job in Calgary, Canada, and moved there with her mother, brother and one sister. She began attending a Vietnamese refugee church and studied hard to complete her high school education. For four years she worked for the YMCA, translating and teaching English as a second language to older refugees. Then she took a student loan and studied for another year to become a teacher's aid. During her training Cindy met Christian foreign students who encouraged her to attend a Bible School. In 1988, with God's help in providing the finance, she enrolled at Prairie Bible College.

Money for tuition kept coming through small gifts during the next four years. Like many students at Prairie, Cindy increasingly felt the Lord was calling her to help build his Kingdom around the world. By the time she graduated in 1992 she was convinced she should join Operation Mobilization's ship, the *MV Doulos*. First, however, she had to pay off 7000 dollars in student loans. For the next five months she worked ten hours a day, seven days a week, until she had enough.

Cindy joined the *Doulos* in 1993. Much of her sponsorship for the next two years came through Bible College friends. Cindy served in the ship's book exhibition, helped to arrange travel for crew members and shared her faith with hundreds of people in such places as South Africa, the Middle East, India and Eastern Europe. Best of all were the opportunities to witness to other Vietnamese she met along the way. This, she felt, was why she had been spared: to share the good news of Jesus' love with those who had never had the chance she had.

Cindy returned to Vancouver after finishing her ship commitment, fired with ideas for the future. She had learned a lot in 'God's navy'. Perhaps she should re-enlist for two more years. Or perhaps she should do what Chinese believers she had met on the *Doulos* had urged: study the Mandarin language in mainland China, and do more ministry among the Chinese.

But when an opening came to go back to Vietnam as a teacher, she knew it was the right direction. Although the government still restricted all religious activity, a vibrant, witnessing church was emerging from the years of persecution. She wanted to be part of helping it grow.

In a plane that flew her effortlessly over the vast body of water she had once crossed in an open boat, Cindy offered a heartfelt prayer of thanksgiving. She had been born into a Buddhist family, and her parents' business back in Vietnam had been to make and sell idols. If she hadn't heard the radio broadcast in the refugee camp she might never have gone to Canada and never learned about Christ. She would have lived with her aunt's family, who were all still Buddhists. But God had kept his hand on her. And now she had come full circle.

Cindy smiled, remembering the words that she had chosen as her personal motto: 'Who knows but that you have come into the Kingdom for such a time as this?' (Esth. 5:14, New King James). 'Use me, Lord,' she breathed, 'just as you used Esther. Please help me bring hope and healing to my people. For without you, I can do nothing!'

VITAL STATISTICS: Girl Soldiers

- Tens of thousands of girls are among the 300 000 children fighting in today's armed conflicts at any one time. Some of them carry a fully-automatic assault weapon by the age of seven or eight.

Children are sometimes called the *'invisible soldiers'* because governments deny they exist, they are kept out of media attention and often end up vanishing – either killed, maimed or abandoned.

> **One fourteen-year-old girl abducted to serve a rebel group in Sierra Leone said, 'I've seen people get their hands cut off, a ten-year-old girl raped and then die, and so many men and women burned alive . . . So many times I just cried inside my heart because I didn't dare cry out loud.'[1]**

WHY GIRLS?

Both boys and girls are generally useful for *cooking, fetching water* and *washing clothes* for an army. They can also *carry supplies and equipment*. But adolescent girls may be handed over to rebel fighters as *wives or sex slaves*.

Increasing numbers of girls go into *actual combat*. Cambodia's Khmer Rouge put them at the front to take the worst of the fighting. Or girls are sent into enemy territory to act as *human mine detectors or spies*.

Susan, a sixteen-year-old Ugandan abductee, told of her experience: 'One boy tried to escape, but he was caught . . . His hands were tied, and then they made us, the other new captives, kill him with a stick. I felt sick. I knew this boy from before. We were from the same village. I refused to kill him and they told me they would shoot me. They pointed a gun at me, so I had to do it. The boy was asking me, *"Why are you doing this?"* I said I had no choice. After we killed him, they made us smear his blood on our arms . . . They said we had to do this so we would not fear death and so we would not try to escape . . . I still dream about the boy from my village that I killed. I see him in my dreams, and he is talking to me and saying I killed him for nothing, and I am crying.'[2]

HOW ARE GIRLS RECRUITED?

Some governments make it compulsory for under-eighteens to serve in their military forces. These include countries that signed the UN's Optional Protocol against this practice in 2002. In Yemen, the military age is fourteen. Almost half of Bolivia's armed forces are under eighteen. Children in some places have been shot for trying to escape recruitment.

Rebel groups abduct many thousands from their homes or right off the street, or press-gang them. In Burma, whole groups of children from the ages of fifteen to seventeen years old have been surrounded in their schools and forcibly conscripted.[3]

Destitute parents may give or sell their daughters to armed groups. According to a study in Sierra Leone, 'many mothers have remarked on the joy of seeing their ten-year-old dressed in brand new military attire, carrying an AK-47. For some families the looted property that child soldiers brought home further convinced them of the need to send more children to the war front to augment scarce income.'[4]

A significant number of girls volunteer. They may be idealistically motivated, or they may want to get revenge for violence done to their families. Others volunteer to escape abuse or exploitation at home. Some girls simply embrace it to be fed and clothed. In Sierra Leone, one young female member of the rebel army explained: 'They offered me a choice of shoes and dresses. I never had decent shoes before.'

THE CONSEQUENCES

Child soldiers are deprived of their childhood, normal social interaction and educational opportunities. The traumas they experience often leave them with long-term guilt, shame, low self-esteem, nightmares and depression. Trained to

forget home and family, some never find their way back to
their villages. Girls who do are likely to be rejected as
'spoiled', whether they were forcibly conscripted or not.

Children wounded in combat may be abandoned, or
unable to get adequate medical treatment. Loss of limbs or
deafness and blindness are most common. A high number of
girls who have suffered sexual violence are left with Aids or
other diseases. Some have the additional care of babies, who
are also stigmatized. Few countries that have ex-child
soldiers are equipped to deal with such problems.

Sudan is recognized as having one of the worst records of
child soldiers, forcibly recruiting many thousands as young
as twelve. **Northern Uganda**'s ill-named 'Lord's Resistance
Army' has systematically abducted over 20,000 children
through the last seventeen years; figures show 5000 girls in
the last year alone. In 2003, forty-five children were
drowned when they were forced into a river to test its depth.

One-third of child soldiers in **El Salvador, Ethiopia,
Eritrea** and **Uganda** are girls. So are 30–40 per cent of child
combatants in **Angola** and **Sierra Leone,** and 10 per cent in
Kurdistan. The Shining Path in **Peru** is reported to have one
of the largest female contingents of any armed group in the
world. And in **Sri Lanka**, young Tamil girls, often orphans,
have been systematically conscripted by Tamil Tiger
opposition fighters since the mid-1980s. Their most recent
recruitment drives in schools have focused on girls.[5]

**In February 2002 the Optional Protocol to the UN
Convention on the Rights of the Child in armed
conflict came into force. The treaty raises the age of
compulsory participation in armed conflicts from
fifteen to eighteen. This represents a significant
advance in the protection of children's rights.**

**To see which governments have not yet ratified this
agreement, check the Amnesty International website
listed in Appendix 2.**

Notes

1 'Girls With Guns: An agenda on child soldiers for "Beijing Plus Five"', Coalition to Stop the Use of Child Soldiers, UK, {http:// www.child-soldiers.orgs}.
2 'Girls With Guns: An agenda on child soldiers for Beijing Plus Five', UK.
3 'The Invisible Soldiers: Child Combatants', *The Defence Monitor*, Center for Defense Information, July 1997.
4 'The Invisible Soldiers: Child Combatants', July 1997.
5 Afua Twum-Danso, 'Africa's Young Soldiers: The Co-option of Childhood', published in Monograph No 82, April 2003.

VITAL STATISTICS: Health – Life expectancy

WORLDWIDE

Around 1.3 billion people have no access to clean water. Every eight seconds a child dies from a water-related disease. Dirty water kills 3 to 4 million men, women and children annually.[1]

- Tuberculosis is the single biggest killer of young women worldwide. Over 900 million females, most between the ages of fifteen and forty-four are infected; 1 million will die and 2.5 million more will get sick this year. In some parts of the world, the stigma attached to TB leads to isolation, abandonment and divorce.[2]
- About 200 million people around the globe are infected with a parasitic disease called **schistosomiasis (or bilharzias)**, caused by infested surface water. Twenty million suffer severe consequences such as renal failure or bladder cancer. The disease is endemic in 76 countries.[3]

Vitamin D deficiency affects the growth of 30 per cent of children in China, South Asia and Africa, also reducing their resistance to disease. Over 25 per cent of Chinese children and 37 per cent of Mongolian children have been diagnosed with rickets of varying degrees.[4]

- *At least 250,000 young children lose their sight each year because of the lack of a small amount of vitamin A in their diet.*

Over 30 per cent of the world's population – over two billion people – are anaemic, mainly due to iron deficiency. Severe iron deficiency anaemia is causing the deaths of an estimated 50,000 women a year during childbirth.[5]

- **Iodine deficiency** in pregnancy is causing as many as 20 million babies a year to be born mentally impaired.[6]

CLOSE-UP

- **Afghanistan:** The life expectancy of women is forty-six years. There are 16,000 maternal deaths annually, making maternal mortality one of the second highest rates in the world. Only 12 per cent of women have access to obstetric care. Afghan women also suffer the highest rate of tuberculosis in the world, 70 per cent of cases occurring during fertility.[7] About 70 per cent of the population are undernourished, and only 13 per cent have access to treated safe water.[8]
- **China:** The neglect of female offspring is dramatically evident. According to the World Health Organization, 'In many cases, mothers are more likely to bring their male children to health centres – particularly to private physicians – and they may be treated at an earlier stage of disease than girls.'[9]
- **India:** In many Indian homes, women are the last members of the family to eat. Often they survive on leftovers. According to UNICEF 47 per cent of children under three are malnourished, *and 50 per cent of women are anaemic.*
- *Yemen:* Two-thirds of children with malnutrition are girls.
- *Zambia:* One in five children die before their fifth birthday.

LIFE EXPECTANCY FOR WOMEN BASED ON 2003 ESTIMATES			
Ten lowest countries		Ten highest countries	
Country	Age (years)	Country	Age (years)
Mozambique	31.6	Andorra	86.6
Botswana	32.3	San Marino	85.3
Zambia	35.3	Macau	84.8
Lesotho	37.1	Japan	84.4
Angola	37.8	Canada	83.4
Swaziland	37.9	Monaco	83.4
Zimbabwe	37.9	France	83.1
Malawi	38.3	Guernsey	83.1
Rwanda	40.2	Australia	83.1
Namibia	41.2	Switzerland	83.0

Source: CIA World Factbook, *Washington, DC: Central Intelligence Agency, 2003.*

INFANT MORTALITY

- **Mozambique** has 199 infant deaths per 1000 births, followed by **Angola** with 193.8 and **Sierra Leone** with 146.9. Compare these high death rates with countries such as Japan – only 3.3 infant deaths per 1000 births, Sweden and Iceland, which have 3.4 and 3.5 infant deaths per 1000, respectively.
- **Malaria** takes the lives of almost 3000 African children each day. A very-low-income African family might spend 19 dollars a year for malaria treatment out of a yearly income of 68 dollars. Malarial anaemia is estimated to cause as many as 10,000 maternal deaths each year.

> **Diarrhoea has killed more children in the past ten years than all the people killed by armed conflicts since World War II. Nearly 7000 children die each day due to dehydration caused by diarrhoea.**

Notes

1 Peter H. Gleick, 'Dirty water: estimated deaths from water-related diseases 2000–2020', *Pacific Institute Research Report*, 15th August 2002.
2 'TB Advocacy, A Practical Guide', WHO Global Tuberculosis Program.
3 Disease Fact Sheet: Schistosomiasis. See: {http://www.worldwaterday.org/2001/disease/schistosomiasis.html}.
4 See UNICEF website: {http://www.unicef.org/infobycountry/china.html}.
5 UNICEF press release, 24th January 2004.
6 UNICEF press release, 24th January 2004.
7 Lynn Amowitz and Vincent Iacopino, Asia Source, 'Health and Human Rights in Afghanistan', 6th November 2003.
8 UN News Center, 6th November 2003.
9 Joseph Farah, 'Cover-up of China's gender-cide', Western JournalismCenter/FreeRepublic, 29th September 1997.

VITAL STATISTICS: Health – Aids

Many men in Africa and Asia believe that sexual relations
with a virgin can cure the virus that causes Aids. This has
led to a tragic increase of infection among young girls. For
every HIV-positive male there are six infected females.

**More than 16.4 million women today have contracted
HIV or Aids. Last year 1.3 million women died from
Aids-related illnesses.**

- In sub-Saharan Africa, teenage girls are five times more
  likely to get Aids than boys, since girls are mostly infected
  by older men.
- In the last three years the total percentage of women
  infected by Aids has risen from 41 per cent to 47 per cent.
- In sub-Saharan Africa 55 per cent of all HIV-positive
  adults are women.
- Uganda has one of the most comprehensive prevention
  programmes in Africa. Infection rates among educated
  women dropped by more than 50 per cent between 1995
  and 1997.
- In Africa and Asia, early marriage forces young girls to
  have sex when their bodies are not fully developed. This
  makes them vulnerable to tearing and abrasions, which
  can lead to HIV infection.
- Many believe that women with any knowledge of sex
  before marriage indicates she is a 'bad' woman. But lack
  of knowledge can be fatal.
- In Senegal, men who were surveyed believed that female
  circumcision is advantageous as it 'rationalizes women's
  desire and helps women resist men'. Female circumcision
  increases women's risk of contracting HIV or Aids.
- Transmission of Aids from men to women is twice as
  likely than from women to men. The risk is especially
  high in the case of unwilling sex with an infected partner,
  since condom use is unlikely.

- Violence such as trafficking, forced prostitution, incest and rape – including marital rape – all put women and girls at risk of contracting HIV.
- HIV-positive women are subjected to violence, even murder. Sometimes they are physically and emotionally abused when their positive status is revealed.[1]

Notes

1 UNIFEM Fact Sheet on Gender and HIV/Aids, UNAIDS 'Report on the Global HIV/Aids Epidemic', June 2000; UNAIDS 'AIDS Epidemic Update' December 2000, UNICEF 'Progress of Nations 2000' and UNIFEM pilot studies.

Chapter 6

For their sake becoming poor

'Give all to love; obey thy heart. Friends, kindred,
days, estate, good fame, plans, credit
and the Muse – nothing refuse.'
Ralph Waldo Emerson

It was almost love at first sight when sixteen-year-old Ruth met Stefan – tall, blonde and two years older than she was. By the end of their holiday at the youth camp in the north of Germany they agreed that a longer relationship would only make sense if they had marriage in mind. Their love for Jesus and for each other sustained them through the next seven and a half years, while Ruth attended a Bible School and Stefan studied theology. In 1987 they were at last united in marriage. The newly wed Mr and Mrs Wagner moved to Stefan's home city of Bonn to work in a church, supremely happy. Still, Ruth never forgot God's clear call on her heart. At the age of seventeen she had pledged to take the news of his redeeming love to people who had little chance of hearing it, where there were few missionaries. Stefan shared the same burden. As they prayed together through the countries listed in *Operation World* it soon became evident where the needs were most urgent.

Already familiar with Operation Mobilization, they contacted the German office to say they wanted to serve somewhere in the Arab world. The office suggested Egypt since the team there offered a good two-year training program on language and culture. This seemed like a sensible idea. After two years they could always return to Europe for Stefan to earn his master's degree. But those two years in the field stretched into two more and then a commitment to stay indefinitely. Egypt was where God wanted them.

Ruth was twenty-five when the couple first left Germany in 1989. She and Stefan had been married only a year and a half. Once, during their dating days, Stefan had asked Ruth if she would be willing to share a very simple lifestyle with him. Both young people had grown up in upper-class families and knew little of real want. Ruth thought about it. Although she had no clue then of what might lie ahead, she answered in the affirmative. If God led the way, she would be willing to give up a life of comfort.

But their first exposure to the back streets of Cairo was a shock. They had committed themselves not only to working with the very poor but to living among them. Ruth's heart sank as they walked through tiny alleyways off crowded streets, choked by heat, noise, dust and unpleasant smells. The reality of their mission hit home.

The first place they settled on could have been worse, they agreed. They were young and without children; everything was still a great adventure. But by the end of five months they realized they weren't really living like the poor. Since their landlord wanted them to leave any-way, they found other accommodation: eighteen square metres on the ground floor of a decrepit five-floor build-ing. The apartment consisted of one tiny room for sleep-ing, a sitting area, bathroom and kitchen. No windows lit the interior and it was very damp. But most of the other landlords they had met were unwilling to rent to foreigners, suspicious of their reasons for choosing to live in such conditions. So the couple had taken the place out of desperation.

The next year was Stefan and Ruth's true baptism by fire. Although they installed a window for more light before they moved in, the sewage problem was appalling. The overloaded main pipe in their street that was meant to serve far fewer than the actual four hundred residents, periodically clogged up. When the upstairs tenants used their sink or toilet the water had nowhere to go, and overflowed into their toilet. Sometimes the flood was so bad they were forced to shovel sludge into the street, or use their window for an exit instead of the door. Their landlady refused to do anything about it, merely suggesting they put stones in front of the door to stop the mess from going further. Sick at heart, Ruth sat on her sofa and cried. To make matters worse she contracted hepatitis and was confined to bed for a month.

Team members all learned to soak fruits and vegetables they bought from the bazaar in bleach. In spite of precautions, however, diarrhoea was a common presence in their home, as it was all over the Arab world. Dust coupled with erratic availability of water and electricity meant that Ruth was forced to give up her high standards of housecleaning. During the summer, water didn't flow from the pipes until midnight or soon after, so women had to do their washing and cleaning then, and store water for the next day. Mail came once a month, by special arrangement. Listening to BBC news on the radio was their main link to the outside world.

In time the Wagners were able to move upstairs in their building; here they lived for nine more years. But the landlady remained a constant thorn in the flesh, demanding the foreigners' exclusive attention and screaming abuse if they visited anyone else. Since they wanted to make as many friends as possible the situation was uneasy, to say the least. Could the woman be troubled by an evil spirit?

One time while Stefan was attending meetings in another country, the floor in one of their rooms collapsed. The metal rods holding it up had rusted away. The landlady blamed the Wagners, insisting that a leak from their ancient washing machine had caused the damage. Ruth lost control of her temper and shut the door in the woman's face – a deadly offence in the Arab world. She repented later, of course, but by then the account of Ruth's actions had been spread far and wide.

Stefan's and Ruth's parents visited them during their first year. They were appalled by the living conditions, and pleaded with the couple not to try to raise children in such a place. Others back home agreed. But in time Ruth was happy to discover she was pregnant. She returned to Germany two months before the baby's birth, and the arrival of dainty Angelika aroused even stronger opposition to the Wagner's lifestyle. How could responsible parents even consider exposing a baby to such hazards, friends argued?

But Stefan and Ruth took little Angelika back to Cairo when she was three months old. No one could love their daughter more, but they were convinced that the God who called them could be trusted to care for her. Of course, having a family altered their situation considerably. Ruth found herself wading through a whole new sea of traditions and superstitions governing child-care in Egypt. Everything she did for the baby was examined, commented upon and criticized. Even nappies were a great curiosity. And of course, visitors to the Wagner's home carefully refrained from expressing admiration for the newborn. Everyone knew that praise for anything of value was a sure way to draw the evil eye. Amulets were almost universally worn – blue beads pinned onto babies' clothing – to fend off the power of jealous ill-wishing. The Wagners had to accustom themselves to friends dutifully declaring how ugly Angelika was.

But one of Ruth's greatest tests of faith came when Angelika contracted amoebic dysentery. Angelika had begun to crawl by then, putting things into her mouth. It was also possible that she had swallowed a neighbour's tap water. Ruth resisted having to give her baby strong medication, but amoebas had to be treated.

Later, when Angelika kept screaming instead of falling asleep, she sought a local friend's advice.

'Your baby is too tense,' the neighbour pronounced, 'why not try a body massage massage to help her relax?'

Ruth watched as a local woman expertly rubbed Angelika with oil from head to foot. To her surprise, the little girl fell into a merciful sleep. But then the old lady took her into her arms and began to recite verses from the Qur'an.

Alarmed, Ruth snatched back her baby and went home, weeping. What if the woman's chanting had somehow harmed Angelika? What had she done? Stefan's response was calm but firm. Either they totally believed that God could protect them and their children, he told her, or they should go back to Germany.

Ruth knew he was right. The next day she returned to the old woman and asked her to massage Angelika once again. But this time, she added, she would be the one to pray for her daughter. The woman agreed.

Gradually, as the family grew with another daughter and a son born to the Wagners in 1992 and 1995, they found themselves better accepted by the community. Ruth slowly built good relationships with the women on her street, even though this meant keeping her door open to callers at all hours, no matter how inconvenient this was.

Privacy was not an option. She and Stefan were watched continuously. Everyone knew exactly what they ate, what they wore and what they bought. One neighbour even went through their waste to see what they threw away.

One day each week the family got together with the rest of the team for discussion, prayer and fellowship. Meetings were held in another part of the city so everyone could enjoy relative freedom. As always when she left her neighbourhood, Ruth wore a long *jalabayah* – a loose covering garment over other clothes – and a headscarf. Dressing like the women around her was essential for acceptance. And a headscarf communicated that she was 'religious'. Western women were widely judged on the basis of their movie and TV image, and considered morally corrupt. Ruth felt she needed all the help she could get.

The Wagners set aside another day in each week for personal rest and recreation. Before the children came along, they treated themselves to sitting in the luxurious lobby of one of Cairo's five-star hotels, writing letters and drinking coffee. With children they had to be more inventive. Sometimes they went to a sports club. Swimming pools required membership, which was expensive. But they could take an occasional sail on the Nile and visit an ice cream shop or a fun fair.

Stefan and Ruth were soon made to realize that Egyptians and Europeans had very different attitudes about child discipline. Neighbours were horrified if the Wagners scolded or corrected their little ones for misbehaving. Arabic culture dictated that children could more or less do as they pleased until they went to school and had to conform to rules.

But as the years passed they saw Angelika, then Annelie and their son Markus grow up happy, healthy and well-adjusted. Even from back home, criticism of the

Wagners' unusual lifestyle was heard less often. The children attended a good school for families of foreign workers. Later they went to a German school. Far from being deprived, the three benefited from international playmates and learned to speak Arabic, German and English. Although they still considered themselves to be German by nationality, there was a lot of Egyptian evident in them as well. They were always happy to return to friends in Cairo after intervals in Germany. The only thing they did sometimes miss, they admitted, was the greenness and comparative cleanness of the European countryside.

But God had a way of surprising the family with special gifts when they most needed them. One exceedingly hot summer during the children's school holiday, acquaintances in Cairo asked if the Wagners would house sit for them. The house was outside the city, with a garden and even a swimming pool: a lifesaver in temperatures that reached over 40 degrees Celsius.

When the Wagners felt the need for a longer break after ten years, they opted to stay in Jordan rather than Europe. A year away from the Arab culture would make re-entry to Egypt more difficult, they reasoned. So the family found a house with a big garden in a village outside Amman. Everyone enjoyed the change.

Stefan and Ruth never doubted that their long-term ministry among the destitute was a specialized calling. Only workers who were certain of God's leading could persevere. Even then, they could easily burn out if they were not careful. 'Success' in such a ministry was hard to measure. Even years of total immersion – dressing, speaking, eating and living just like their neighbours – did not guarantee tangible results.

Ruth faced the fact that most of the women in their neighbourhood were less interested in religion than in sheer survival. Many appliances and labour-saving devices were unknown in the cramped and crumbling quarters that littered vast areas of Cairo. As one woman told her, 'Religion is for the men in the mosque. What does it have to do with me?'

Occult practices, on the other hand, were part of the fabric of everyday life. 'Folk Islam' prevailed. So did superstition and fear. Ruth knew women who felt themselves to be demon-possessed. In these cases they dressed like a bride and threw a party, dancing until they fell into a trance-like state. Then a chicken would be slaughtered over their heads, covering them with blood. In this way a woman made peace with the demon. Curses were also common. When a pregnant friend found water sprinkled in front of her door, she was convinced a curse had been left to cause a miscarriage.

An estimated 90 per cent of Egyptian girls undergo female genital mutilation. Although this practice is not ordered or even mentioned in the Qur'an, few religious leaders oppose it and some actively support female circumcision. Little girls as young as five undergo the 'surgery' by knives, razor blades or scissors, often without anaesthetic in the belief that it will preserve their virtue. Each year, some of these victims bleed to death. Others suffer prolonged infection, or face a lifetime of complications.

With childbearing considered the primary purpose for a woman's existence, most girls marry young. Single girls and even childless married women receive little social respect. When a woman gives birth, preferably to a son, she is awarded the title '*Om*' meaning 'mother of', followed by the child's name. This shows she has fulfilled her calling. A childless woman might even choose to be called 'mother of the absent one'[1] rather than suffer the shame of using her own name.

Over time, Ruth gained the respect of her neighbours by patiently listening to their problems, providing practical help and even sharing the food she cooked. A few times, during the month of Ramadan, they gave a family a chicken to eat, the only meat they had all year because of their extreme poverty. The Wagners kept the fast but made sure they told people it was not a way of earning favour, to get them into heaven. Sometimes her friends were willing to listen to her talk about spiritual things. Other times she could only offer to pray for a sick person or a specific problem. Only once when she asked if she could pray in Jesus' name did a woman turn her down.

Her joy overflowed when a friend eventually asked Jesus into her life. A team member led another woman to the Lord, and Ruth later helped to disciple her. The two became good friends. Amira had suffered many years of physical and verbal abuse from her husband. As the beatings got worse, she decided she could endure no more and applied for a divorce. But at the court hearing her husband told the judge she was a loose woman, often coming home late at night. To the false accusations he added a true one: that Amira had converted to Christianity.

Amira knew what this could mean. She might be turned over to the State Security Police, who were known to imprison and even torture people. Her only desire at this point was to drop the case. Her husband knew he had her, and forced Amira to give him a large amount of money in return for her freedom. Her own family cut her off. Still, she refused to deny her love for Jesus Christ. 'He is my greatest treasure,' she told Ruth and Stefan. 'How could I let go of him?'

Presenting a consistent witness in their adopted culture was a daily challenge. Even a small incident, like the time Ruth discovered the theft of her perfume by a neighbour's girl, highlighted the pitfalls. Ruth cared more about the perfume's emotional significance than the expense of the gift itself. She wanted it back, but the situation was delicate. A confrontation with the girl would end their friendship – and any relationship with her family. Honour was everything in this society. To dishonour a person by exposing them brought shame upon their whole family, and was considered worse than the act of misconduct itself. In fact, tradition dictated that God only judged a person for a sin if he or she was 'caught in the act'. The logic was that if he already protected the person from discovery and punishment on earth, he would continue to do so for eternity.

When the girl in question passed their apartment later on, Ruth opened the door to the distinct fragrance of her missing perfume. She solved the problem by going to her neighbour's apartment during the girl's absence, and asking her mother for the bottle that her daughter had 'borrowed' earlier. No problem. Ruth got her gift back and the girl got the message without their relationship being destroyed.

But mistakes were also made. Always having to consciously decide the right thing to wear or say or do was exhausting. And the bottom line was that no matter how much she and Stefan tried to identify with the people, they were still regarded as foreigners. Once or twice they had been dismayed when 'friends' who seemed to respond to the gospel suddenly disappeared from worship times, probably because they were police informants. Worse were the times when other members of their team were arrested and deported. It also hurt when another Christian organization or and even an Egyptian pastor undercut their efforts, by trying to lure new believers away from their fellowship. Ruth admits there were moments when she was ready to pack up and leave.

The couple knew there was always a possibility the decision could be taken out of their hands. A current of fundamentalism ran through Egypt that was deeper than the Nile. Those who did not conform to Islam attracted unwelcome attention.

After attending a conference in 2002, Stefan re-entered the country and presented his passport at airport immigration. The officials refused him entry. After grilling him like a common criminal, police put him on a plane to Germany. Ruth and the rest of the team were stunned. Suddenly the whole of the family's care and other responsibilities were on her shoulders. The children were in the middle of their school year. Should she take them out and leave Egypt? Was God telling them it was time to move on, or was this just a temporary roadblock from Satan? Stefan was convinced it was the latter. They could not abandon their newborn fellowship of believers. Men and women were meeting together for the first time, and only a complete family could host such meetings. He flew to Jordan, seeking another way into Egypt.

Ruth and the children visited him there, but two months passed before they were finally reunited once more in Cairo. Friends, co-workers and believers saw this as God's direct intervention. But the whole situation had shaken them. Other workers were also being refused entry. It was apparent that the pressure was on to block Christian efforts. With time running out, the Wagners knew the priority was to see their little fellowship firmly established. They also needed to identify and train an Egyptian leader. 'Before long you'll need to stand on your own in your faith in Christ,' they told believing friends. 'Get used to the thought.'

Later that year the mission asked if the Wagners would pray about taking over the leadership of a European office. Sadly accepting that their days in Egypt were numbered, they were able to see the move as God's answer. It was time to bring closure, at least for the present.

Not, of course, that they would ever forget the land or the people that had become so much a part of them. Just as the Lord had long ago led Joseph to the land of the pharaohs to fulfil his purposes, so he had led them. And if he chose, he could one day lead the Wagner family back again. It was all up to him.

Notes

1 Or *Om Mohammed.*

VITAL STATISTICS: Honour killings – Getting away with murder

More than 13 women each day – 5000 a year – die in 'honour killings' worldwide. These daughters and wives are murdered because their male relatives consider behaviour such as dating, talking to men or even cooking badly immoral. In places where men go unpunished for overtly illicit relationships, women die for the faintest rumour of impropriety. Even victims of rape may be despatched by families who feel they've been shamed. Although such killings occur most often in the Middle East, residents in many other countries regard the practice as necessary to preserving the family honour.

- An **Egyptian** bride was attacked by her father on honeymoon for marrying a man he didn't approve of. After cutting off her head, he proudly paraded it down the street.[1]
- A mother in **Pakistan** was sleeping next to her three-month-old baby when her husband shot and killed her. A neighbour had informed him he'd seen a man near the field where she was working.[2]
- A girl in **Iraqi Kurdistan** was set afire by her husband because she went to her brother-in-law's wedding party without her husband's permission. She died after a month of anguish.[3]
- A young woman in **Jordan** ran away to marry the man she loved without the family's permission. A few years later her sister ran away to join her. Their brothers found out where the girls were living, went into their home with axes and hacked both sisters to death. The incident came only a day after Jordan's parliament rejected a bill that would impose tougher sentences for such crimes.[4]
- Some Jordanian women have chosen to remain in prison after serving their sentences, rather than return home and face violence or death at the hands of their families.

- In the **UK**, honour killings also hit the headlines in 2003 when a twenty-two-year-old Pakistani bride was stabbed to death on her wedding day. At least one woman a month dies from an honour killing in Britain. The perpetrators are prosecuted. In other countries, killers generally receive a light sentence or none at all.[5]
- 'Every year about 40 **Palestinian** women die at the hands of their fathers or brothers,' writes Geraldine Brooks in *Nine Parts of Desire*; 'they are accused of pre-marital or extra-marital sex. Often the women are then burned so the killing is passed off as an accident. The killer becomes a local hero.'[6]
- **Pakistan**'s Human Rights Commission reported that at least 461 women *in two provinces alone* died at the hands of family members in 2002. Around 372 were known to have been killed in 2001. The commission added that the actual number of victims was probably closer to 800. The death rate is growing, as women seeking divorce from abusive husbands trigger deadly attacks.

When a Pakistani man was tried for the murder of his wife's lover, the judge quoted the verse from the Qur'an that establishes men as the *'custodians of women'*. It was explained that a man who kills another man for defiling the honour of his wife or daughter is protecting his property and acting in self-defence. The judge ruled that the appellant – as the custodian of the honour of his wife – had the right to kill the deceased while he was engaged in a sexual act with his wife.

Notes

1 Abu-Nasr, 'Death for Dishonor: Women Slain for Perceived Wrongs', *The Press Enterprise*, California, July 2000.
2 Abu-Nasr, 'Death for Dishonor: Women Slain for Perceived Wrongs', July 2000.
3 'Honour Killing: Catalogue of Horror in Iraqi Kurdistan', compiled by The Independent Organisation of Women in Sulaymaniya, Iraqi Kurdistan.
4 'Fresh "honour killing" in Jordan', *BBC News*, 10th September 2003.
5 *WorldNetDaily*, 9th November 2003.
6 Geraldine Brooks, *Nine Parts of Desire* (New York, Doubleday, 1995), p. 49.

VITAL STATISTICS: Honour killings – Laws

Extracts of Penal Codes in Arab States regarding 'Crimes of Honour'[1]

Algeria: *Article 279 Penal Code*
Murder, wounding and beating shall be subject to excuse if committed by one spouse against the other spouse or against his/her partner at the moment of surprising them in the act of adultery.

Iraq: *RCC Resolutions no. 49 and 6 of 2001*
Absolutely absolves from liability a man who kills or attempts to kill another who has raped or forced a blood relative of the killer to have sexual intercourse with him. Further and by way of protection to the killer, should he become the victim of revenge, such revenge will be deemed an aggravating circumstance.

Provides that when a man kills his wife or a blood relative by reason of a crime of honour, and then kills another person who taunts the killer and imputes dishonour, then the second crime will be deemed to be subject to an extenuating circumstance. Any one who kills the said killer will be subject to a death sentence.

Jordan: *Article 340 Penal Code*
He who discovers his wife or one of his female unlawfuls committing adultery with another and kills, wounds, or injures one or both of them, is exempt from any penalty. He who catches his wife, or one of his female ascendants or descendants or sisters with another in an unlawful bed and he kills or wounds or injures one or both of them, benefits from a reduction in penalty.

Kuwait: *Article 153 Penal Code*
He who surprises his wife in the act of adultery or surprises his daughter, mother or sister in the act of sexual intercourse with a man, and immediately kills her, the man or both of

them, shall be punished by prison for a period not more than 3 years and a fine of not more than 3000 *dinars* (amount to be verified) or by one of these two penalties.

Libya: *Article 375 Penal Code*
Whosoever surprises his wife, daughter, sister or mother in the act of adultery or in illegitimate sexual intercourse and immediately kills her/her partner or both in response to the assault that has affected his *sharaf* or the honour of his family, shall be punished by a prison sentence. If the act leads to grave or serious injury of the said persons in these circumstances, the penalty shall be prison for not more than two years. Mere beating or light injury in such circumstances shall not be penalised.

Morocco: *Article 418 Penal Code*
Murder, injury and beating are excusable if they are committed by a husband on his wife as well as the accomplice at the moment in which he surprises them in the act of adultery.

Oman: *Article 252 Penal Code*
He who surprises his wife committing adultery or surprises his mother, sister or daughter in an unlawful bed, and immediately kills or injures her or kills or injures the person committing adultery with her, or kills or injures both of them, may be exempted from liability or be liable to a reduced penalty according to the provisions of article 109 of this law which is printed below.

> *Article 109:* In the case of exemption liability there shall be no penalty, while in the case of liability to a lesser penalty [in view of extenuating circumstances] the penalty shall be reduced as follows:
> 1. If the action is a felony giving rise to the capital punishment or life imprisonment it shall be reduced to prison for at least one year.
> 2. If the action is another felony it shall be reduced to prison for six months to one year.

Syria: *Article 548 Penal Code*

1. He who catches his wife or one of his female relatives committing adultery or illegitimate sexual acts with another and he killed or injured one or both of them benefits from an exemption of penalty.

2. He who catches his wife or one of his ascendants, descendants or sister in a 'suspicious' state with another benefits from a reduction of penalty.

Yemen: *Article 232 of law no. 12 of 1994*

If a husband kills his wife and whoever is with her at the moment of their adultery or if he attacks them in a manner that leads to death or disability, no option of *qisas* arises; the husband shall be penalised by imprisonment for a period of not more than one year or by a fine. This ruling applies also to a person who surprises one of his female relations in the act of illicit fornication.

'But the Lord is still in his holy temple; he still rules from heaven. He closely watches everything that happens here on earth. He puts the righteous and the wicked to the test; he hates those loving violence.' Ps. 11:4,5 Living Bible

Notes

1 Lynn Welchman, 'Extracted provisions from the penal codes of Arab states relevant to "crimes of honor"'. See {http://www.soas.ac.uk/honourcrimes/Mat ArabLaws.htm}.

VITAL STATISTICS: Inequalities

Statistics show that in no region of the world are women and men equal in legal, social or economic rights.

EMPLOYMENT OPPORTUNITIES

WOMEN'S WAGES IN MANUFACTURING CALCULATED AS A PERCENTAGE OF MEN'S WAGES IN THE SAME JOB

Country	Percentage (%)
Japan	59
Brazil	61
Mexico	70
USA	76
Netherlands	78
Turkey	97

PERCENTAGE OF WOMEN AMONG ADMINISTRATIVE AND MANAGERIAL WORKERS

Country	Percentage (%)
Korea	4
Turkey	6
Spain	12
South Africa	19
Germany	19
USA	44
Sweden	59

Source: United Nations, *The World's Women, Trends and Statistics*, (New York: United Nations, 2002).

- Women make up two-thirds of the world's work force, yet earn one-tenth of the world's income and hold only 1 per cent of total assets.

INEQUALITIES UNDER ISLAM

Adultery

Iranian law reads: *'The stoning of an adulterer, or adulteress will be carried on while each is placed in a hole and covered with soil –**he** up to his waist, and **she** up to the line above her breast'* (emphasis added).

Under Islamic law, if you can escape and run away you are allowed to go free. Obviously no woman can escape if she is buried almost to her neck!

Heaven and hell

'Whereas out of every thousand men only one will go to hell. Yet, out of every thousand women only one will be found in heaven.'

Mohammed said, *'I was shown the Hellfire and that the majority of its dwellers are women.'*

These statements are *Hadiths* – part of the Traditions rather than the Qur'an itself – but still highly respected, recording what the Prophet is reputed to have said or done or permitted. In all writings, the delights of Paradise are mostly promised to faithful men. As a result many Muslim women live in fear of death.

Inheritance

'To the male a portion equal to that of two females,' Surah 4:11, the Qur'an.

This statement indicates a daughter should receive only half the inheritance of her brother. When a woman's husband dies she receives only a quarter of the legacy. If there are several wives they divide the quarter.

Prayer and fasting

Iranian girls of nine years are expected to rise for dawn prayers and fast during Ramadan. Boys are not required to fast or pray until they are fifteen.

Clothing restrictions

The Qur'an does not require women to be completely veiled
or secluded. Each Muslim culture imposes its own dress code
or *hijab* for females, ranging from a simple headscarf to an
all-enveloping head-to-toe cloak or *burqa*, like those worn in
Afghanistan. Extremely conservative Egyptian women even
wear gloves. Interestingly, little attention is given to modesty
for men, although the Prophet Muhammad instructed that
they should cover themselves 'from navel to knee.'

Among North Africa's Tuareg people it is the male, not
female, who veils his face to prevent the enemy from knowing
what he's thinking. Women, say the men, have nothing to
hide. Most Muslims disregard this custom, however, since in
Arabic, 'tuareg' means 'the abandoned of God'.

Saudi Arabia's rules for women's attire are so stringent
that in 2002 religious police stopped schoolgirls from fleeing
their burning school building because they weren't wearing
the proper headscarves and robes. One witness said he saw
three policemen beating students who tried to leave. Fifteen
girls died in the blaze.[1]

Several cases have also been reported of acid thrown in
the faces of unveiled women by extremists in parts of
Pakistan and Afghanistan. While many Muslim women
would defend veiling, others deplore being forced to cover
themselves.

Voting rights

In November 1999, Kuwait's National Assembly rejected by
a two-thirds majority a decree by the Emir that would have
granted women the right to vote and run for political office.

Witness

In most situations in a court of law, two women witnesses
are required in contrast to only one male.

Notes

1 BBC News, 'Saudi Police "Stopped" Fire Rescue', 15th March 2002.

Chapter 7

Into India

*'There is no limit to what can be accomplished
if it doesn't matter who gets the credit.'*
Ralph Waldo Emerson

At nineteen, Canadian Janice Ross couldn't wait any longer to 'do life'. She had always been a sickly child, in and out of hospital and spending long periods in bed. Now it was time to seize the adventures she'd always craved. The army, she decided, would provide just the ticket.

To everyone's surprise the teenager survived training camp with flying colours, and after training as a book-keeper she was shipped out. Five years of various assignments ended with a six-month stint at the United Nations in Israel and Egypt. She celebrated her discharge by setting off to see the rest of the world, paying her way with any job she could find. For the next ten years she worked as a nanny in Germany, cooked on a ship in Australia, waitressed in a Swiss ski resort and clerked in an office in England.

Her parents kept praying for her. Back when Janice was born prematurely and struggling for life, her father had laid his hands on the incubator and told God that if he saved this child, he would dedicate her to his service. It was a promise he had never shared with his daughter throughout all her years of wandering from God. But when she finally returned to Ontario, practical problems drove her back to the family home. And walking through the doors of her old church she was surprised – and moved – by the warm welcome they gave a long-lost sheep. Her rebellion began to fade. Could it be that in running away from Jesus Christ, she had missed out on the most important thing life had to offer? Janice's surrender was unconditional.

During her teen years she had been fascinated by Israel and the Jewish people, reading books about the holocaust and trying in vain to understand how such a thing could happen. Why hadn't Christians done more to save the Jews? Why hadn't God intervened? Reading the news about modern-day conflicts like the Yom Kippur War, she was amazed at Israel's survival. Her six months stationed in Egypt and Israel made a deep impact as she saw the country with her own eyes.

Later, while working for two years as a nanny in Munich, Janice's best friends were Israeli university students. Now that she knew the truth, the apostle Paul's heart cry for the Jews became her own. She was heartsick that she had never shared *Yeshua* – Jesus – with her Israeli friends. But perhaps she could still befriend Jews in Canada.

Janice signed up for Hebrew lessons in a local synagogue. Later she heard about Jews for Jesus, and joined them for her first-ever public attempts at evangelism. As her love for Jewish people grew, so did the idea of returning to Israel. She thought of applying to her denomination's mission board but they had no evangelistic outreach to Israel. Then, in an Operation Mobilization newsletter, she read about the need for a bookkeeper in their Israel office. Although she wanted to do evangelism she saw this as God opening the door.

Janice spent her next five years serving with a very different army. From the very beginning, her duties in the office were incidental to sharing about Christ. She was in Israel long-term. Everything in her life had been pushing her towards these people. Not even threats by neighbouring Arab nations and suicide bombers could put her off.

During the Feast of Tabernacles celebrations, Janice was part of a special evangelism outreach in the ancient seaside city of Akko. Every year, thousands of Israelis gather in this port for an open-air arts festival. The OM team boldly sang their own songs of witness, and within four days gave out 7000 Christian books. One of the men they talked to put his faith in Christ.

Janice was astonished to meet Israelis who were wearing the Hindu dot or *tikka* on their foreheads. Some were selling Indian clothes and jewellery. Was there such a thing as Hindu Jews? Researching the subject she learned that after finishing their compulsory army service, many Israeli young people went overseas for a taste of freedom and adventure before settling down. South America and Asia, especially India, were popular destinations. In 1997, 16,000 Israelis were travelling to India; by the year 2000 the number had increased to 60,000. In fact, 60 per cent of students in one of India's Buddhist centres were Israelis. Some of these young people became gurus then returned to Israel to set up their own communities and attract their own followers. Their influence was enormous.

Janice began to meet Israelis who had been spiritually and physically damaged in India, mostly through drugs. She heard tragic stories of accidents: of young people who ended up in hospital or prison, or who had simply disappeared entirely. The desire to help these travellers remained in her heart. Nobody seemed to be doing anything.

In March of 1999, Janice went with a small team on a five-week survey trip to India. They had done their homework and knew that Israelis rarely travel alone but in 'waves'. The groups tended to congregate in the same locations and take over area hotels and restaurants. Often they had a bad reputation with local Indian residents; they were only tolerated for the income they brought. Janice's team saw beaches and restaurants in the southern state of Goa catering for hundreds, even thousands of Israelis staying for extended periods during the winter. Many hotels even had signs and menus printed in Hebrew. When summer came the wave would move on to the cooler northern state of Himachal Pradesh, where marijuana grows wild on the hills. Some of the travellers settled there permanently, enticed by the comparatively low cost of living.

Everything the team saw confirmed the tales they had heard in Israel. They were stricken by the young people's obvious fascination with Hinduism and Buddhism. Drug-taking and psychedelic trance parties were popular features of their Indian lifestyle. On nights that the moon was full, revellers headed for the beach to dance for hours on end. A Shiva idol presided over an 'altar' belting out loud, pulsating music. The cocktail of music, LSD, ecstasy and marijuana sent many of the dancers into a trance. Others partied through the night.

Janice's team met Indian Christians who had a genuine concern for these lost children of Israel. The believers told them they had been praying for a long time that God would send the right workers. To Janice, this was the final confirmation. She could speak Hebrew as well as

English, and her own army experience had given her a sympathetic understanding of these travellers. One of the Messianic congregations back in Israel had even offered to help support her. With the approval of OM in both India and Israel, Janice began searching for like-minded people to pioneer a new ministry. A South African couple joined her and they set off for India in October 1999, just in time for the November to February 'high season' for travellers.

Unfortunately, the team fell apart only a few weeks after arriving in the subcontinent. Andriette became ill and discovered she was pregnant and so she and Eric decided they should return home. Janice searched for a place to stay on her own in Goa, and prayed for rein-forcements. God supplied temporary help at unexpected times during the next year: a couple living in Goa, several Swedish volunteers at a Christian Ashram, a retired Dutch couple and a single woman from Finland. A few of the Indian believers also got involved, and the church she attended there gladly prayed and helped her give out tracts at Christmas.

Janice kept in regular touch with prayer partners through e-mail. In January 2000 she jubilantly announced a breakthrough: the last-minute cancellation of the biggest trance party in history, scheduled for the eve of the new millennium. Goa's newly elected chief minister was a strong opponent to drug dealing and took position just in time to get the courts to intervene. This was a thrilling answer to prayer.

Of course there were plenty of discouragements as well. Many of the Israelis visiting India were tourists. Even those who came searching for spiritual truths were not always ready to consider the claims of Jesus. Janice looked for creative ways to share without being consi-dered a *'nudnik'* or jerk and God blessed her efforts. The ministry obviously had potential. All she needed was co-workers!

A café that was popular with Israeli travellers in Goa became one of Janice's regular stops. Once she and a friend met a group of Israeli men and an American girl, eating a last meal in the restaurant before heading for Thailand. As they chatted, Janice prayed for a good opening to lead the conversation on to spiritual lines. The opportunity came when the Israelis started smoking hashish. One of the men held the *chillum* (hookah or pipe) up to his forehead before smoking, and Janice challenged him. He knew that this was a traditional gesture to honour Shiva – not only the Hindu god of destruction but also the god of drugs. How could he, as a Jew, honour Hindu gods, when the God of Judaism hated idolatry?

'When in Rome do as the Romans do,' one of his friends grinned and shrugged.

But Janice wouldn't accept this. Did being in Rome mean adopting Rome's pagan religious practices, she asked? It emerged that the leader of this group had been raised in a famous ultra-orthodox Israeli family. His father was a rabbi, and he was fed up with religion and God. Janice told him she was sorry he'd had a bad experience. She had no wish to argue or add to his hurt, but maintained that the one true God was wonderful and well worth knowing. After a long discussion, the men accepted a booklet from her to read on their way to Thailand.

Janice took a short break back in Canada early in 2000, but six weeks later she was back on Indian soil. Though still without a team, she was no less determined to follow the 'travellers' trail' to the north. Once she arrived in the city of Manali, Himalchal Pradesh, she planned to live in a place of her own.

The valley of Manali was surrounded by glorious, white-capped mountain peaks and fruit trees white with blossoms. Unfortunately, the house Janice found to rent was not quite so impressive. The place had been unoccupied for a year and required a major spring cleaning as well as repairs. Insects abounded; none of the flying cockroaches that she had encountered in the south, but plenty of fleas as well as spiders that left a rash after crawling on her skin. But Janice soon had the house tidied up.

Her days fell into a routine. After starting out with personal devotions at around half past seven in the morning, she would head – somewhat tentatively – into the kitchen for breakfast. A screen around her cupboard was supposed to keep out bugs and rats, but both still managed to eat her vegetables. If a rodent had been caught in a trap, she and the landlord generally released it a safe distance away.

Following breakfast she heated water for a wash (that is, if there was no power failure, which there was almost every day). The house only had cold running water that needed to be boiled for drinking. To heat it for laundry, dishes and bathing she filled up a bucket and stuck in an electric coil, taking care not to shock herself. The process of heating water, washing clothes in the bucket, rinsing and wringing each article out by hand took several hours. To take a bath she sat on a low bench and washed herself from the bucket.

Next in her routine came ministry preparation, or else she took a fifteen-minute hike down to the village to try to send e-mails. Often the connection to the server was down, or her messages were cut off while uploading or downloading. Since this might happen up to twenty times in a single hour the process called for a great deal of grace. While she was in the village she bought fresh food. With no refrigerator, shopping had to be done almost daily. She might also choose to have lunch and visit friends before returning home to do a number of tasks:

working on the computer, making Bible verse posters to put up and practicing new chords on her guitar. An after supper activity might be reading her Bible or other books from the local church library, before going to bed. The higher altitude took a toll on her body and she found she needed more sleep than usual.

In spite of this rather monastic schedule, Janice assured her friends by e-mail that she wasn't lonely:

> Not many Israelis come yet, but they soon will. I don't quite know how to go about sharing as I am by myself, but I spend quite a lot of time in prayer and asking God for wisdom. I don't know why I don't have any other team members yet but I really believe I should be here, and in my weakness somehow God will be glorified. It doesn't matter if things start slow, as long as the Lord builds the house.

As Janice persevered she discovered that many travellers grew tired of eating in restaurants and were glad to be invited to a home-cooked meal. Sitting around the table afterwards, the group often fell into a deep discussion about their faith.

After the first spring and summer in the Himalayas, Janice had to exit the country again to renew her six-month visa. This became a regular pattern through the next years, and she made the most of these opportunities to share and recruit in other countries. This time she headed to Israel. Her visit happened to coincide with a three-day New Age festival being held during the Jewish New Year, in the valley of Armageddon. About 15 000 people were expected. Janice thought it sounded like a good place to do some evangelism, and went with a small team. The experience left her shaken.

'It was the most appalling thing I've ever seen,' she wrote. 'In India, young Israelis who are usually atheists or agnostics get into Hinduism or Buddhism. As if that's not bad enough, they've then brought these religions back to Israel, added a bit of tradition, and made them the new Judaism.'

On New Year's Eve Janice listened to the lyrics of a song being sung on the main stage: 'I was travelling, I didn't care about the way . . . Then I found out, God is one.' The words encouraged her a little. Perhaps there *were* some religious Jews at the festival. But then the group went on to sing about Shiva, the Hindu god of destruction and regeneration, and his consort god, Parvati. Janice asked one of the workers by the sound booth if she had heard correctly.

'Yes! God is one,' he explained, 'Elohim, Shiva, Parvati, Buddha are one, and we are one with them.'

Later Janice watched aghast as hundreds of Israelis – ultra-Orthodox Jews among them – faced the sun and prayed for the spirit of the east to fill them. Ironically, that same weekend, violent riots broke out between Jews and Arabs in Israel, the West Bank and Gaza. To Janice it was history repeating itself: as if God was allowing his people to be attacked, as they had in Old Testament times because they had turned away to worship idols and false gods.[1]

New Age festivals have proven to be a popular way of marketing eastern ideas in Israel. In 2002 Janice attended a six-day 'Boombamela,' a take-off of the giant Hindu 'Kumbamela'. Advertising the event were posters depicting a drugged Indian guru with a star of David on his forehead. Janice's team camped on a beach with thousands of other participants, talking, praying and inviting people to meals. Every kind of mysticism was on show: yoga, meditation, reiki, crystals, native American and Eastern religions, Hari Krishna and Jewish cults. They saw naked men wearing nothing but body paint from head to toe wandering through the crowds while trance music blared and drugs flowed freely. But Jesus was there, too, searching for his lost sheep. The team won favour with the owner of a big tea tent who allowed them to sing and play the guitar. Festival-goers actually walked up to them and asked for a New Testament. They were even invited to give a concert on the main music stage. The Word of God was amplified to many thousands.

Whenever she is in Israel Janice also seizes openings to explain her work to Messianic congregations and youth groups. Her goal is always to form more partnerships and excite believers to pray or join her in India. As a result, her solitary eight months in 2000 was followed by only a single night alone the successive year. Soon after that, a committee of Israeli and Scandinavian believers met with Janice and proposed sending small teams to work with her on an ongoing program. Each group of two or three people would go through a preliminary month of training in Jerusalem before spending four months in India. To Janice it sounded like her dream was coming true at last.

During trips to Israel Janice visits some of the travellers she has met previously in India. One person she had kept in touch with was Sharon. Sharon had overdosed on drugs and suffered a breakdown in Manali. Janice and friends had stayed with her until her father arrived to take her home. It was good to see Sharon again, and to meet other members of the family. The girl was better but still on medication, and Janice was disturbed to hear the girl talk about going back to India. She decided to share more of her own personal testimony.

Several other Israelis she had met in Manali were now living in the Tel Aviv area. When Janice went to see them, she realized that recent terrorist attacks on friends and neighbours had left them deeply shocked. One girl,

Maital, had hidden under a restaurant table when shooting began nearby. Although she wasn't yet ready to accept a New Testament from Janice, she listened to her carefully. So did Gadi and Hadass, who took her out to dinner in appreciation for her friendship and help in Manali. Occasionally Janice is able to link such friends with believers in the area.

Visa breaks in Canada are also spent informing others about her ministry. In 2001, a month or two after the September 11th terrorist attack she was invited to spend a few weeks in New York City, with Jews for Jesus. Their commitment encouraged her. Going with a team to 'Ground Zero' to witness and distribute tracts was something she would not forget.

Sometimes flights to and from India offered stopovers in Thailand. Janice took these opportunities to explore the Israeli situation in this country. Drug use wasn't as conspicuous among the waves of travellers in Thailand, she discovered, because of the strict penalties. But alcohol was everywhere, and trance parties were just as popular. Janice talked to many young people and realized there was a big potential for ministry to Israelis in Thailand, if only the workers could be found.

During one stay in Bangkok Janice noticed a poster in her guesthouse urging guests to visit American inmates in Thai prisons. Most were serving long sentences for drug trafficking. Janice and a friend found their way to the notorious Bangkwang prison, known as the 'Bangkok Hilton'. Here almost 7000 prisoners languished in almost inhuman conditions, in space meant for half that number. Diseases such as TB and Aids were endemic. The girls were allowed inside without much difficulty. While her friend went to talk to a Dutch prisoner, Janice spent some time with Christopher, a thirty-one-year-old American. Chris had already served five years of a nine-year

sentence. His mother and sister had visited occasionally,
he told her. The US embassy had also sent him magazines
at first, although this small comfort had now stopped.
Christopher had just finished a month in solitary confine-
ment and was surprised but grateful that someone had
come to see him. During their conversation he mentioned
that he had once gone to church back home. Janice
resolved that she would at least get a Bible to him.

Just at that moment she spotted an older man on
his way to visit someone, carrying something. It was a
Bible. She went to talk with him, hoping he could give
Christopher a copy and visit him, but to her dismay
the man was a Jehovah's Witness. The experience grieved
Janice. If only more believers in Bangkok would visit
these men and women who were slowly wasting
away behind bars. When she and her friend got back to
town they made another poster to urge people to visit
prisoners.

During a later stop in Thailand, Janice was delighted to
make contact with Thai believers who ran a Christian
Prison Ministry. Over the years they have seen ten
thousand men and women come to faith in fifty-three
prisons around the country. Their big need is for English
speakers who can help teach inmates the English language,
using the Bible. Janice and her team were pleased to take
part in a meeting for five hundred prisoners.

Janice has also explored opportunities for reaching
Israelis in the Hindu Kingdom of Nepal. Surprisingly,
before the Maoist uprising reduced numbers, Kathmandu
used to host the biggest Passover *Seder* (feast) in the
world with almost 1500 coming from Israel. While she
was in the city Janice came upon many men and women
she knew. God gave her the chance to deepen friendships
and share his truth. But once again she was appalled by
the easy availability of drugs. Just walking around a

tourist area for an hour and a half one day, she was approached by eight different dealers.

Janice is now forty-something. She has no illusions about the hazards of what she is attempting. Apart from the challenges of daily life and the instability of the company she keeps, there is very real danger of escalating hostility between India and Pakistan. She and other workers have made contingency plans 'just in case'. But she has no wish to abandon her mission.

'God has been working in me my whole life to get this together,' she reflects. 'Even the "wasted years" of travelling have given me a certain credibility with those I meet. I've shed a few tears of frustration, I can tell you, but just when I really feel fed up with myself, God does something great.' A smile lights her face, and she adds, 'These people are too precious to God for him to let me screw it up. They've lived through so much and they're dying out there. So he is going to do it!'

Notes

1 See for example 2 Kings 17: 7–23 or Jeremiah 1: 14–16.

VITAL STATISTICS: Marriage – Child brides

> According to the World Health Organization, pregnancy-related deaths are the leading cause of death worldwide for girls fifteen to nineteen years old.

Maternal mortality is 5 times higher for girls under fifteen years of age, and twice as high for fifteen to nineteen-year-olds.[1] Miscarriages and stillbirths are also much more likely. Besides the obvious health hazards, child brides are deprived of educational opportunities and the chance of a normal childhood.

INTO THE MUSLIM WORLD

Around many parts of the Muslim world it is not uncommon for girls as young as nine to be married to men old enough to be their grandfathers. While the practice may be officially illegal, it is accepted because the Prophet Muhammad himself set the precedent. At the age of fifty-two he took a six-year-old child as one of his wives; the marriage was sexually consummated when she was nine.[2]

- *Iran:* The legal age for marriage was raised from nine to thirteen in 2002.
- *Bangladesh:* The legal ban on the marriage of girls below eighteen years of age has rarely been enforced. About 51 per cent are married by the age of eighteen. According to estimates by groups campaigning against the practice, under-age nuptials make up at least a tenth of the nearly two million weddings every year in the nation of more than 130 million people. Many of these brides are just ten years old.[3]
- *Niger:* A recent UNICEF study found 44 per cent of women aged between twenty and twenty-four had been married under the age of fifteen. Child brides of eleven and twelve are increasingly the victims of financial, moral

and traditional pressures. Tens of thousands of girls disappear each year into arranged marriages that were once thought to be a thing of the past.[4]

- *Nigeria*: Forced marriages are common, particularly in the Muslim north. Some estimates say that 37 per cent of girls aged fifteen to nineteen are forced to wed.

- *Pakistan:* Almost 68 per cent of Pakistan's population resides in rural areas, and many girls between twelve and fourteen are either pregnant or already mothers. To circumvent the law, parents record their daughter's age as sixteen on the marriage certificate. Since the birth certificate is not yet a legal requirement for marriages in Pakistan, there is no way to check falsification of age.[5]

PAKISTAN'S 'MARRIAGE ACT'

A law passed under the military dictatorship of Zia ul-Haq in 1985 rules that if a non-Muslim woman converts to Islam, her previous marriage is null and void. Radical Muslims see this law as an invitation to kidnap, rape and bully Christian women and girls into converting to Islam. They are then forced to marry their Muslim captors, who claim that their parents and husbands have lost all right to the abducted women and girls. Through indifference, agreement or fear, most local police simply go along with it.[6]

In February 2001, Naira Nadia, a fourteen-year-old Christian girl, was kidnapped and gang raped by a group of Muslim men after she shared her faith with school friends. The men forcibly converted her to Islam and sent her parents a certificate of conversion. Despite evidence that Naira was under age and therefore could not marry or convert to another faith without her parents' consent, the presiding judge at Lahore High Court ruled in favour of the abductor. Naira has been missing for almost seventeen months. Her family filed an appeal to the Supreme Court in February this year, but they are under increasing pressure from local Muslims to drop the case.[7]

According to a survey the incidents of rape of Christian women by Muslims, registered with the police, climbed to 780 in 2002. Actual numbers are much higher. Most girls and women in this culture choose to keep silent, as reporting an assault would bring shame to their families and keep them from finding a husband.[8]

INTO THE HINDU WORLD

● *India:* Eighteen is the minimum age for a woman to marry but under-age brides remain a tradition. A 1998–99 National Family Health Survey found one-third of all adolescent girls are married by the age of fifteen. In northern states such as eastern Uttar Pradesh, marriages are arranged for girls as young as a few months to eight years old. The brides remain in their maternal homes until they attain puberty; then they are dispatched to their marital homes.[9]

In Rajasthan, where early marriages are also common, not all families are prepared to wait for puberty. In many cases documented by sociologists, girls as young as six or seven have been taken away by their husband's families to begin working as servants or field hands. Many husbands reportedly tire of their marriages after the third, fourth or fifth child, when their wives are still teenagers.[10]

North America
● *USA:* The Fundamentalist Church of Jesus Christ of Latter Day Saints (FLDS) is a sect that broke from the Mormon Church 70 years ago in bitter disagreement about the practice of plural marriage, polygamy and under-age brides as young as fourteen. About 6000 followers live in communities in Arizona and Utah. A report in *The Arizona Republic* newspaper related that many young men in these communities have been encouraged to leave, sometimes under pressure from a church-controlled police force, so older religious leaders can woo teen brides more easily.

> The FLDS teaches that the only way a man can reach the highest level of heaven is to take at least three wives in this life. Even though polygamy is against the law in Utah and unconstitutional in Arizona, FLDS members have never tried to cover up their lifestyle.[11]

Notes

1 'The reality of adolescent girls' lives', {http://www.iwhc.org/uploads/RealityAdoGirlsLives.pdf}.
2 'Muhammed, Aisha, Islam and Child Brides', {http://www.answering-islam.org.uk/Silas/childbrides.htm}.
3 Tabibul Islam, 'Bangladesh's child brides face health problems', 22nd May 2000.
4 Boureima Hama, 'Niger's child brides are back, trading dolls for babies', *Africa News*, 6th June 2002.
5 Ameena Khan, 'The Plight of the Girl-Child in Pakistan', *Child Workers in Asia*, Vol. 16 No. 2 May–August 2000.
6 *Christianity Today*, 21st May 2001.
7 *Worthy News*, (Internet News Service) October 2003.
8 *Pakistan Christian* Post, 6th October 2003.
9 Ammu Joseph, {http://www.reportingpeople.org} 2nd October 2003.
10 John Burn, 'Child Marriages, Though Illegal, Persist in India', *NY Times on the Web*, 11th May 1998.
11 Joseph A. Reaves and Mark Shaffer, *The Arizona Republic*, 28th September 2003.

VITAL STATISTICS: Marriage – Brides at risk

Every year up to 25 000 brides are deliberately set on fire in India and Bangladesh. In the capital city of Delhi alone, a woman is burned to death every twelve hours. Most of their murders go unpunished.

BRIDE BURNING

India: The dowry system has been legally banned in India for over forty years. Nevertheless, the offering and receiving of a marriage settlement is still an expected practice in many parts of the subcontinent. Since it falls upon the bride's family to come up with large amounts of money or valuables (averaging today the equivalent of five times the family's annual income), it is unsurprising when a female birth is hailed with dread. In fact, the dowry system is a direct cause for the escalating rates of infanticide (see Vital Statistics: Female infanticide). Some girls, knowing their fathers are unable to pay a bride price, have been known to commit suicide.

Sparks may fly after a marriage if the groom's family decides they want more than the previously agreed-upon dowry. They may try extortion, and if her family cannot meet their demands, the bride is in danger of abuse, divorce and even death.

Indian wives who are battered have few options. If they are very lucky their families will take them back, but often parents cannot or will not allow daughters to return because of the social stigma. India offers few government shelters for abused women. Those that do exist have such an appalling reputation that women would rather suffer the blows of their husband or in-laws.

Ironically, death rates have increased as India becomes more prosperous. Officially recorded fatalities shot up from

1912 in 1987 to 4006 in 1989 and 6222 in 2000. Most of the victims were burned to death. Members of the husband's family pour kerosene oil over the bride and set her afire, hoping the incident will pass for a suicide or an accident with the kitchen stove. Other women have been burned with acid. But the statistics cited are only the official figures. Thousands of deaths go unrecorded, and only about 3 per cent of perpetrators receive justice.[1]

Bangladesh: Although the bridegroom bears the responsibility for providing nuptial gifts in Muslim cultures, dowry is so much in demand in Bangladesh that many poor families are unable to get their daughters married. According to one report nearly 50,000 girls from one district alone have no hope of wedding because of the inability to meet dowry demands. In another district, 2500 marriages ended in divorce in 1999 because of dowry-related feuds. But 2026 women lost their lives between 1990 and 1997 according to the Women and Child Affairs Ministry of Bangladesh. The Bangladesh National Women Lawyers Association says that 203 women were killed and 34 tortured for dowry by their in-laws in 2000.[2]

Pakistan: According to the country's Progressive Women's Association, burning accounts for the violent death of at least 300 women each year, most often at the hands of their husbands or husbands' families. Again, police are usually told the victim was killed by an exploding stove, and there is no prosecution. While divorce is possible in Pakistan, some families apparently decide to rid themselves of unwanted wives by murdering them.[3]

'BRIDES OF THE QUR'AN'

Her wedding day has arrived. Friends and relatives of the young bride-to-be chatter as they prepare her for the ceremony. The girl is bathed and carefully dressed in finest silk and jewels, then hours are devoted to the

artful arrangement of her hair and application of make up. Finally the bride-to-be is led forth. The ceremony proceeds. She places her hand on the holy book of Islam and repeats her vows. She is now a married woman.

Except that she has no husband.

Her parents have just followed a very old practice accepted in the rural Sind areas of Pakistan. Marriage to the Qur'an is an ingenious way of marrying a daughter whilst keeping the family line pure and its wealth intact. The girl in question may be only ten or fifteen years old, but the ceremony remains binding for the rest of her life. The 'bride' is now kept in seclusion. Contact is forbidden with any male over fourteen years old, including immediate family members. In some cases she is not even allowed to see a man on TV.

Husbandless wives like these may try to fill the endless hours by studying the Qur'an. Small wonder that some of the brides – estimated to number about 3000 – eventually go mad.

In the book, *Why I Am Not A Muslim*, author Ibn Warraq quotes one woman relegated to this fate: 'I wish I had been born when the Arabs buried their daughters alive. Even that would have been better than this torture.'[4]

BRIDE SELLING

China's 'one child' policy, which encourages the choosing of boys over girls, has led to a severe distortion of the male to female ratio. Millions of marriageable men cannot find wives. Criminal gangs and marriage brokers – essentially slave dealers – search the countryside, kidnapping and buying women and girls to offer to prospective husbands. Women often co-operate with a marriage broker in the hope of saving their families from hunger. Chinese authorities have freed an average of 8000 kidnapped women and girls every year since 1990. But kidnapping continues to grow as a multi-million dollar industry.[5]

MAIL ORDER BRIDES

Search the subject *'mail order brides'* on the internet and you will find over a hundred thousand sites offering e-brides. Some specialize by nationalities, others boast a 'warehouse' of available women. Customers on the high end of the scale may take arranged trips to various countries and bring their brides home. While men and women have undoubtedly made happy matches this way, many thousands of women have ended up trapped in violently abusive relationships. Should battered immigrant wives dare protest, they are threatened with deportation. Differences in language and culture often exacerbate the situation. While this industry cannot be called 'trafficking' because it is done with consent, it is largely unregulated and produces an increasing number of victims worldwide.

MARRIAGES OF CONVENIENCE

The Shiite followers of Islam (the majority of whom live in Iran) are allowed a unique form of marriage that may last from a few minutes to as long as ninety years. In most cases the *muta'a* arrangement is simply legalized prostitution. A man and woman sign a contract to come together for a specified time. Usually the man agrees to provide some financial benefit. The contract is then recorded and sanctioned by a cleric. Men may take as many temporary wives as they like. A woman, however, may only have one husband at a time, in order to establish parentage in case she becomes pregnant. Any child born from such a union will be raised by the man and his permanent wife.

Since this practice has official religious approval it is not considered sinful. Nobody has to have a guilty conscience. Temporary marriages are quite normal in Iran; young men are even counselled to regard it as an outlet for their sexual urges, until the time they are ready to establish a permanent marriage. In Iraq, the

> practice was banned under Saddam Hussein but has
> now returned. Huge numbers of widows see it as the
> only way to survive. Clerics who support *muta'a* say it
> offers them sexual and financial freedom.

Notes

1 Usha Rai, 'Dowry: South Asian Malady,' Women's Feature Service, {http://www.JANMANCH.org}.
2 Usha Rai, 'Dowry: South Asian Malady', {http://www.JANMANCH.org}.
3 BBC News Online, 27th August 1999.
4 Ibn Warraq, *Why I Am Not A Muslim*, (New York, Prometheus, 1995).
5 Liu Bohonhg and Dorinda Elliott, 'Trying to Stand on Two Feet', *Newsweek*, 29th June 1998.

VITAL STATISTICS: On the streets

There are probably over *100 million children* working on the streets. Approximately *1 million more* are forced into the sex trade worldwide every year. The average age keeps decreasing and even very small girls and babies are involved.

NORTH AMERICA

USA: Between 300,000 to 600,000 juveniles are engaged in prostitution. Girls are increasingly younger, dropping from fourteen to thirteen years of age and even twelve. Each year between 1.2 and 2 million teenagers hit the street – runaways and 'throwaways' – and half of them will turn to prostitution to survive.

Canada: Social workers in Toronto estimate that there are 10,000 children living on the streets, and that many of them fall prey to pimps. More than 400 children, some as young as eleven, are reported as working for pimps in Calgary and 300 to 600 in Montreal. Hundreds of children are being abused as prostitutes in the province of British Columbia, which has the highest incidence of child prostitution in Canada.

EUROPE

Half a million girls and women from Central and Eastern Europe now serve as prostitutes in European Union nations.

Czech/German border: A 2003 UNICEF reporter found that bus stops, petrol stations and rest stops on the German–Czech border area had been converted into 'bazaars' where child prostitutes meet mainly German men. Children and infants from across Eastern Europe are sold into sex slavery by their families. A German authority estimated about 100,000 German sex tourists travel to the Czech Republic, about half of whom are interested in children.[1]

Greece: The number of minor children in the sex trade has tripled during the last five or six years. Prostitution is legal in this country.

Great Britain: In Bradford, children as young as eleven have been enslaved for prostitution. One survey showed that the average age of one hundred teenage girls in touch with social workers was fourteen. Older pimps exploit them, lock them up in bed-sits and often deny them access to food or a toilet. A report by children's charity Barnado's has discovered children as young as twelve working as prostitutes in Scottish cities.

ASIA

At least a million children are being exploited for sex in Asia. The greatest numbers are in India (500,000), Thailand (60,000–200 000), Taiwan (40,000–60,000) and the Philippines (60 000).

MIDDLE EAST

UAE: An estimated 50 per cent of women in prostitution have been coerced into the sex industry while under the age of consent.

Turkey: There are 60,000 female child prostitutes aged between twelve and seventeen years.

AUSTRALASIA

Australia: Over 3000 children work in the sex industry, some younger than ten. Girls work in brothels and engage in escort work, street prostitution, pornography, sexual favours and stripping. Paedophilia is a serious problem.

Philippines: This is one of the favoured destinations of paedophile sex tourists from Europe and the United States. An estimated 1.5 million street children work as pickpockets, beggars, drug traffickers and prostitutes.

LATIN AMERICA

It is estimated that there are at least *40 million street children* in Latin America. Many are victims of abuse, sometimes murder, by police and other authorities and individuals who are supposed to protect them.

Brazil: Approximately 100,000 street kids between the ages of seven and eighteen.

Mexico: About 5000 girls are currently being used for sex tourism, prostitution and pornography.

Peru: Up to 10,000 street and underprivileged children die in the city of Lima every year.

Notes

1 Benoit Finck, 'Border "haven" for child prostitution', 29th October 2003, {http://www.news.com.au}.

Chapter 8

A little child shall lead them

'We can do no great things,
only small things with great love.'

Mother Teresa

For Nurse Mary Hill of Sault Ste. Marie in Ontario, Canada, it wasn't a bolt of lightning or a voice from heaven that launched her from her comfort zone. She just happened to read about the need for nurses in a children's feeding program in Northern Iraq. After thinking and praying about it for a while, she decided she should take a year's leave of absence and do her bit. After all, one year wasn't a lot to give back to God after all he'd given her. And her job – a well-paid one because of her special field – would still be waiting when she got back.

As it turned out, changes in the Iraq project eventually led her to a vacancy in a Lebanon hospital instead. In January 1997 Mary flew from Canada for an orientation conference in Germany. The temperatures were bitterly cold, and even before travelling on to the snow-covered mountains of Lebanon, she contracted pneumonia. Her suitcase of winter clothing didn't make it until three weeks after she did.

It was not the most promising start. The stark, no-frills nurse's quarters in the hospital outside Beirut had no heat; her teeth chattered so much she didn't know how she was going to survive a day, never mind a whole year. Expatriate mission workers often chose more comfortable housing outside the hospital grounds. But although the dormitory was more of an adjustment, she wanted to feel close to the Lebanese staff. It would be easier to make friends and pick up more of the language from fellow workers. And as Mary admitted to herself, it might also force her to re-evaluate the things she had always considered 'basic' to her lifestyle.

Living in the mountains was certainly much simpler. Although she had none of the time-saving devices she had back home, she had much more time. What a difference it made not to have a car, television or even a phone. And for the first time in eight years she didn't have to carry around a pager. The stillness was refreshing.

So was Lebanon's scenery. Like most newcomers, Mary had heard more about the country's political turmoil than its natural beauty. While the famous cedars of Lebanon were now few and far between, this was still the most densely wooded of all Middle Eastern countries. Her hospital, originally intended to treat TB patients, was built high on a pine-scented mountain. Below her was the Mediterranean coastline that would blossom with fruit trees and flowers during the summer. Though Beirut still bore the scars of the 1975–1990 civil war, it was now a modern and thriving seaport.

Of course, some of the realities that Mary faced were not so wonderful. She was forced to wash all her laundry in a bucket, and clothes strung around her tiny quarters could take as long as a week to dry during the winter months. And since Arabic was the national language, communication could also be frustrating. Mary learned phrases and got by with English, a dash of French and a lot of pantomime.

The biggest disappointment was the inadequate medical facilities. Hamlin Hospital was established by missionaries in the early 1900s, and before the war it had been one of the best TB treatment centres in the Middle East. Several wings of the building, including the nurse's training school, now stood derelict.

Appalled, Mary wasn't sure at first if she could stay. The old people's home adjacent to the hospital had broken windowpanes and windows that wouldn't shut even when it snowed. Temperatures often fell to zero degrees inside, so residents were forced to huddle in coats and hats for warmth. Hot water was only available in a single location. As for equipment, she found only one thermometer to share among twenty-eight residents. Staff accommodation was very basic, though most workers were so anxious to keep their jobs no one dared complain. If they left, a dozen others waited to take their place.

Drawing upon years of specialized training, Mary introduced more professional standards in the nursing home. She also pitched in to clean and paint and give the institutional walls a cheerful facelift with full-colour Scripture posters, lettered in Arabic. Mary's goal was to minister to the spiritual and physical needs of her patients, for many had suffered deeply during the years of war.

Old Abla, for instance, had been forced to go into the home when she developed a heart condition several years before. The illness actually saved her life. During the war her village was attacked. Every resident, her entire family included, were massacred.

At first, working in the old people's section was tough. The place was so bleak and the people so unappealing.

But as Mary heard their stories she found herself beginning to love her patients. She realized that the love wasn't her own, it was the Lord's who had sent her there.

Once a month Mary also travelled out with an Operation Mercy medical team to the Bakaa Valley. Here Lebanon's Bedouin people, forced by law to give up their nomadic lifestyle, lived in desperate hardship. The once-proud people were reduced to scraping a living by hard labour, mostly in other people's fields. On the country's social scale they were at rock bottom, despised and rejected. The medical team did what they could to provide vaccinations and primary health care to children in the Bedouin communities. During the summer, Mary also assisted in running a camp for destitute children from Beirut slums. Sometimes she found herself nursing children who needed specialized care.

Little Fatmi was one of these. Born with a large cleft palate, Fatmi was the fourth child in a family that already had too many mouths to feed. Her home was a hovel and to complicate things, Fatmi's mother was already a diagnosed schizophrenic by the time she was married at fourteen. After the birth the woman seldom picked her baby up or spoke to her, leaving Fatmi to lie neglected and soiled. Feeding was sporadic. By the time she agreed to help from a doctor in the shanty town, Fatmi was thirteen months old and weighed only eleven pounds. The doctor told Mary about the case, hoping she could help. She agreed to nurse the baby until she was strong enough to undergo the cleft palate repair.

Fatmi arrived at Mary's small quarters two days after Christmas. As she took the lice-ridden body in her arms, her nurse's heart contracted. The baby was so weak she could not even hold her head up when she was sitting. One more month, the hospital pediatrician said, and she would have died.

Watching over her tiny patient through the long night hours, Mary asked herself what she hoped to accomplish. Even if she helped Fatmi survive, what kind of future could this child expect? Short-term emergency help wasn't really the answer in such cases. All Mary knew was that she had to give the little girl a chance.

Fatmi responded so well to a nourishing diet that within a month she was able to undergo surgery. However, the cleft in her mouth was so extensive that a second surgery was scheduled for early April 1998. The child's father asked if he could leave her with Mary for the interim, so Mary arranged to extend her leave of absence from her job back in Canada. But before the second operation, the man approached Mary again. Would she consider becoming Fatmi's guardian? He had seen how the little girl thrived; learning to laugh and play and even interact with the elderly people Mary cared for at the hospital.

'Think of the home to which she will have to return,' he said.

After a lot of heart searching and prayer, Mary agreed. 'Perhaps I can't help all the destitute children in the world, but at least I can make a difference to this one,' she thought. The arrangement had to be made official in front of a notary public. However, the notary argued that it was a shameful thing to give a daughter to a Christian: 'You'd never get to see her again,' he warned Fatmi's father. He took fright at this and changed his mind. So after the child recovered from her second surgery, Mary had to take Fatmi home. Leaving her in such squalid surroundings hurt more than she would have believed possible. When she went back to visit two weeks later, the livewire had been replaced by a listless, dirty and vacant-eyed little stranger. Knowing she could do nothing more, Mary decided to return to her job in Canada.

A few months later she received news from the doctor in the shanty town. Fatmi's family had disintegrated, and a divorce was underway. The three oldest children were being put in orphanages. However, no orphanage would take Fatmi at such a young age. Would Mary consider caring for her, and a few other needy children, until they were old enough to be admitted to an orphanage?

Mary considered this plea for several weeks. When she was granted another year's leave of absence she agreed to return to Lebanon in October 1998.

Mary rented a small house in a village, and as the months passed the bond between herself and little Fatmi grew. The lack of calcium in the child's diet during her first year had produced rickets: her small legs were bowed and she had very poor teeth. Mary took her to see an orthopaedic surgeon, and after a diet rich in Vitamin D and calcium Fatmi markedly improved.

That same year Mary took in another severely malnourished little girl whom doctors feared had a serious metabolic disorder. Three of Samira's seven siblings had already died in destitute circumstances. Samira survived, but it broke Mary's heart when it came time to return the baby to the family's cold, dirty shanty in Beirut.

The experience of coping with two small children at once opened Mary's eyes to the stresses of single motherhood. To make matters worse, the Catholic village where they lived had turned their backs on the outsiders. No one would speak to Mary, even when she asked for service in the local supermarket. Men showed up on her doorstep several times and tried to get in. Eventually Mary moved, this time to a Druze village, where she received a warm welcome.

Meanwhile, unwilling to see Fatmi go to an orphanage, Mary approached three Lebanese couples about the possibility of adopting her. Each considered the idea, but eventually decided against it. Mary didn't know what to do next. Could God really be saying he wanted *her* to take responsibility for Fatmi?

After contacting a Canadian lawyer about the legalities, she asked the family if they would consider allowing her to adopt their daughter. They cautiously agreed. Fatmi's father gave Mary legal guardianship for the duration of the adoption process in Lebanon. It was a day to celebrate. Mary decided to add the Western names 'Karen Joy' to the child's Arabic one, in anticipation of their future move to Canada. But as one year stretched into two the complications multiplied and the mountain of paperwork grew higher. Mary extended her time in Lebanon; filling out more forms, praying and refusing to give up.

Two, however, could not live as cheaply as one and Karen's family had never offered help with her support. In the year 2000 Mary decided they would do better to return to hospital accommodation. Their two tiny rooms offered unlimited water supply and twenty-four-hour electricity. On the downside there was no sink, and cooking had to be performed on a hotplate. When the cost of electricity doubled, the hospital asked staff not to use electric heaters. This, of course, made for less than pleasant winters.

Mary worked two days a week in the old people's section. By this time the hospital had almost doubled the number of residents, without adding staff or improving conditions. The Presbyterian Synod who oversaw the place, however, continued to sign for Mary's resident visa year by year. This allowed her to stay in the country, for immigration officials frequently checked her status. Often she would take Karen with her into the wards to keep an eye on her. The little girl was a great favourite with the old people; along with entertaining them she managed to keep herself amused. When she started kindergarten, Mary taught English at the school a few days each week to help offset costs. Kind missionary families with girls a little older than Karen kept them well supplied with lovely clothing, books and toys.

Mary and another nurse assisted Lebanese believers in starting a Kid's Club in the hospital chapel every other Saturday. Within a year, seventy children were crowding in from all over the neighbourhood, and a second club was necessary for teenage girls. The great majority of children were from Druze families, followers of a unique secret religion with its own sacred scriptures. For a thousand years the Druze had resisted Christianity. Mary was amazed to see some who had never before heard of Jesus happily learning Bible songs and stories and memorizing verses. Visits to the children's homes helped to strengthen relationships. So did the short summer camps they held.

The Lord cheered Mary with an unexpected Christmas present in 2001. When she stopped to buy a few groceries one wintery December day, the shopkeeper said that a car was being given away in a promotion. He urged her to put her name and address in the box and she laughingly obeyed. To her total shock she was notified a few days later that she was the winner: the owner of a KIA Sportage! Thrilled at God's provision, she later sold the KIA to the team and they gave her a car more economical for mountain travel.

Mary made sure that Karen saw her brothers and sister when possible. The children were allowed to go to the family 'home' from their orphanages for the summer and school holidays. One weekend she invited them to stay with her and Karen overnight. This proved a disaster. The two boys and little girl tore through the little apartment like cyclones, breaking many of Karen's toys with their rough play, tearing her wading pool to ribbons, even standing on the chairs during meals. By the end of the visit Mary felt like she had been run over by a truck. She wondered belatedly if she should have started with one child at a time!

Karen Joy's cleft palate surgery had left her with a residual need for speech therapy. As she grew old enough for kindergarten it also became apparent that she had learning difficulties. Testing showed the six-year-old had only a three-year-old level of concentration. Delayed development was also reflected in her hyperactivity, which made normal schooling a challenge to both her and her teachers. Acting on the suggestion of a psychologist, Mary hired a woman to stay with Karen in the classroom to help keep her focused and simplify directions.

Mary had hoped they could move to Canada before addressing schooling issues. But the delays and setbacks continued. During the spring of 2002 she and her lawyer had submitted the requisite eighteen documents to the court, and it looked like the adoption might finally go through. Only one document remained to be signed by Muslim authorities. But then the family of Karen's mother stirred up an unexpected dust storm. They were still angry and vindictive about their daughter's divorce by her husband, shameful in Lebanese culture, and were looking for a way to retaliate. The family went to community officials with the claim that Karen's father had sold the child to Mary for 100,000 dollars. Nobody wanted to sign the final adoption paper with these allegations still hanging fire.

Mary was almost in despair. She had not had a holiday in four years and ached to return to Canada. By this time Karen had also finished two years of junior kindergarten; it was time for her to go on to a school willing to give special help for learning disabilities. The only one Mary could find charged 7500 dollars for tuition alone.

Meanwhile, Lebanon's political situation was growing increasingly tense, particularly in the southern part of the country bordering Israel. Nobody was prepared for the murder of a young American named Bonnie Witherall in November 2002. Bonnie had been working in a maternity clinic for Palestinians in the south. Early one morning she opened the doors to a gunman, who fired pointblank into her head. Mary knew Bonnie; knew how much she loved the Lord and the Arab people she served. Since the wars in Afghanistan and Iraq, Christian workers were being targeted in several parts of the Middle East. Everyone wondered who would be next.

The answer came the following March when the family home of another team member was bombed. Tragically, although the family escaped injury, a neighbour friend was killed in the blast that destroyed much of their home. Still, Mary and other co-workers in Lebanon felt they had no choice but to keep going in the direction God was leading them, trusting him for each step.

June 2003 brought Mary a renewed surge of hope. *Karen Joy* got her passport. But before the pair could leave the country, all the adoption documents had to be translated and certified by the Ministry of Foreign Affairs. Mary tried not to get too excited. Another court ruling might still be necessary before she had final custody and the courts were adjourning for the long summer holiday.

With every step forward they seemed to slide two steps back. A lawyer working on the Canadian side of the adoption advised Mary that they would need a home study by a licensed Ontario social worker. At the same time Mary's Canadian driving license was due to expire, and on this occasion it had to be renewed from inside Ontario. Hoping to take care of both things, Mary applied for a tourist visa for Karen. The Canadian government rejected the application.

What to do? The home study problem appeared miraculously solved the next Sunday, when a Christian Ontario social worker 'just happened' to visit Mary's Lebanese church. A major power outage on the east coast of America had meant rescheduling the woman's return ticket, giving her an extra week in Lebanon. She told Mary that she had been praying that God would show her what to do with this window of time. The home study was completed but later rejected by the Ministry in Ontario. The social worker, they said, should have obtained prior permission.

So Mary had to start all over again. At least the Ministry of Transport had agreed to renew her driver's license for another five years.

The option of leaving Lebanon without Karen, even temporarily, was something she dared not contemplate. The visa situation was too precarious. Several of her co-workers had already been refused re-entry. She had to believe that God would make a way where there seemed no way.

Mary went ahead and enrolled Karen Joy at an English-speaking school that claimed to be progressive. The psychologist had promised to find someone to help the child in the classroom in return for a monthly salary, on top of the tuition fee. The help didn't come through, so Mary breathed a sigh of relief when someone else became available. Then, the day before school started, this lady decided to take another job. Both Mary and Karen could have cried. Karen said she could not make it in school without help, and Mary knew she was right.

To add to the pressure, one of Karen's supporters in Canada withdrew. How would they cope financially? Mary put Karen into another school run by evangelicals for children with special needs. Part of the tuition was subsidized from outside the country. To help offset the balance, Mary volunteered to do mending one day a week. She also started using public transport more often. Although Karen can ride in a school van each morning, Mary has to travel thirty treacherous mountain miles each afternoon to pick her up. Then there is Karen's half hour of speech therapy on Mondays. Mary tries to look at the positive side: not only is she saving a few dollars on fuel but she doesn't have to deal with the terrible traffic herself.

Wanting to maximize her time in Lebanon, Mary has continued other ministries like weekly prison visits with a team of other women. The detainees are mostly Sri Lankan, Ethiopian and Filipina maids who have had trouble with their immigration papers. The women are warmly appreciative of the team's Bible stories, crafts and singing. Some of the inmates cherish the Bibles they've received in their own languages. In fact, fights occasionally break out over them: the team can only afford five or six Bibles per 'room', and each of the five rooms averages fifty women.

Sometimes, as this Canadian nurse reflects on the drama of the last six years, even she finds it hard to believe. Certainly she never dreamed that she would still be in Lebanon in 2004, her familiar world turned upside down for the sake of one small child. Hopefully, the end of the long battle is now in sight. But whatever it takes before she can go back to Ontario, Mary Hill is certain that Canada could no longer be 'home' without her little girl. She has learned that God is able to weave even the most confusing threads of life together for the good of those who love him. Ultimately, it will be worth it all.

VITAL STATISTICS: Poverty

Over 1.3 billion people worldwide live in absolute
poverty, living on less than one dollar a day. Of this
number 70 per cent are women.

Half the world – over 3 billion people – live on less
than 2 dollars a day.

- Twenty-four thousand people die daily from hunger.
  Children below five make up three-fourths of this
  number.
- Around 800 million people are chronically
  undernourished; 3 billion do not have access to adequate
  sanitation and 2 billion have no access to electricity.

Women in Africa and Asia walk an average of 6 km to
obtain water. One flush of a toilet uses as much water
as the average person in the developing world uses for
a whole day's washing, cleaning, cooking and
drinking.

Poverty can overtake, no matter how hard you work.
In sub-Saharan Africa, women are responsible for 70 to
80 per cent of household food production. The majority
have a huge proportion of manual jobs, but a very low
percentage of skilled and high-paying work.

The number of rural women living in absolute
poverty has risen by 50 per cent over the last two
decades, as opposed to 30 per cent for men.

- **Latin America** has the highest gap in the world between
  the rich and the poor.
- In the **UK,** the bottom 50 per cent of the population now
  owns only 1 per cent of the wealth, and the inequality
  between rich and poor is increasing. A study published in
  the year 2000 indicated that children in Britain are more
  likely to be born into poverty than anywhere else in the EU.[1]

> **It would take 13 billion dollars a year to end hunger for the earth's poorest citizens. Compare this with the 18 billion dollars that is spent on pet food every year in the United States and Europe.**
>
> *'Defend the cause of the weak and fatherless; maintain the rights of the poor and oppressed. Rescue the weak and needy . . .' Ps. 82:3–4*

Notes

1 Andrew Simms, 'Now for a Maximum Wage', *The Guardian*, 6th August 2003.

VITAL STATISTICS: Refugees

There are many millions of refugees and asylum seekers in the world.
   Twenty-eight million people are displaced inside their own country.

- Eighty per cent of the world's refugees are **women and children.** A large number are widows.
- Women and children are also victims of 80 per cent of wartime deaths by small weapons, far outnumbering military casualties.

'Refugee women and children are increasingly targeted by armed elements for murder, abduction, forced military conscription and gender-based violence. In addition, women and children in conflict settings often face heightened health risks such as disruption of health services, facilitating the transmission of HIV and Aids. Women frequently lack access to safe conditions for childbirth and emergency obstetric care.'[1]

- *Azerbaijan:* The unemployment rate of internally displaced women approaches 80 per cent, even though over one-third have specialized degrees or training.[2] Hundreds if not thousands of women, forced from homes in the Nagorno-Karabakh enclave, have for years lived with their families in derelict railroad cars.
- *Burma (Myanmar)*: Female Burmese refugees have fled to Thailand for 15 years, yet very few living in the camps are protected from abuse under Thai law. Many who have already been sexually abused by Burmese soldiers undergo further violence in refugee camps. Yet a culture of silence ensures that such crimes go unpunished.
- *Britain:* Approximately 30 per cent of all applicants for asylum in Britain are women. Seven out of ten are

unaccompanied by their husbands, although about half are caring for children. One refugee group estimates half of the women have been raped or sexually assaulted before reaching the country. Among single women, almost 40 per cent are mothers involuntarily separated from children.[3]

More than half the group surveyed were suffering from clinical depression, with the same proportion having enormous language difficulties with their doctors. Post-traumatic distress is at the root of much depression, yet it is seldom dealt with. Another factor contributing to discouragement is governmental red tape: many must wait for years before knowing if their application for asylum is accepted. The uncertainty is draining, limiting the newcomers' rights and freedom and making it impossible to fully integrate.

> **Displaced and marginalized women are at particularly high risk of exploitation and domestic abuse. However, in many refugee communities around the world, violence to women often goes ignored by civil authorities. The inaction is justified as 'respecting cultural differences'. As long as male abusers are protected under the guise of political correctness, women do not have anywhere to turn.**

'Lord, you know the hopes of humble people. Surely you will hear their cries and comfort their hearts by helping them. You will be with the orphans and all who are oppressed, so that mere earthly man will terrify them no longer.' *Ps. 10:17–18, The Living Bible*

Notes

1 Darla Silva, 'Washington Liaison: The Women's Commission for Refugee Women and Children', 25th September 2003.
2 'Refugees and Internally Displaced In Azerbaijan', Women's Commission for Refugee Women and Children Report, June 2001.
3 BBC News, 3rd December 2002.

Chapter 9

Home is where the heart is

'Life shrinks or expands according to one's courage.'
Anaïs Nin

Brazil, the fifth largest country in the world, also boasts the largest number of Roman Catholics and spiritists. In fact most Catholics are also spiritists, worshipping both saints and spirits. Half a million mediums live in Brazil. Mara's mother was one of them.

Fortunately, Mrs Antonia belonged to the more moderate 'white table' variety of spiritism. The 'black table' of Candomble and Umbanda mixes more deeply and darkly with black magic. Although Mara and her four sisters and brother were never forced to attend meetings, they often went along.

Mara left home at sixteen to attend high school in the state capital, Goias. Students who went were better prepared to pass the very competitive university entrance exams and Mara was determined to earn a university degree. During her last year she went to a private high school in order to fully concentrate on her studies.

This self-imposed isolation left her feeling lonely, however. She sensed something was missing in her life. A visit to a black table spiritist centre only left her more dissatisfied.

Some of the girls in her class were Christians. Occasionally Mara accepted a few invitations to their Youth For Christ meetings, but she wasn't interested in becoming a 'believer'. All the Christians she knew refused to drink, smoke or dance, and she loved to party! The YFC girls even dressed differently. Some believers she knew wore only skirts and refused to cut their hair. Mara decided she would postpone being religious until she was an old lady.

But then she had a dream: the same dream repeated three times. A person she recognized as Jesus Christ was returning to the world with great glory to take away his followers. There was a sound of singing and great celebration as everyone left with him. Everyone except Mara. She was left behind. The dream disturbed her. She tried to brush it away but couldn't.

When the YFC girls invited her to a camp, Mara at first refused. She was so sick of studying, however, that she changed her mind. The camp was not the fun and games she hoped for, but a retreat with lots of Bible teaching and meetings. At the end of the weekend a friend asked Mara if she wanted to respond and ask Jesus into her life. She did.

For a while after that her life changed radically. She bought a Bible and tried to do everything that was expected: giving up drinking, dancing and smoking – even wearing conservative clothes. But it was too much, too soon. Less than a year after she was accepted to the university she was back to her old habits, avoiding Christian friends. She even joined the crowds at the notorious annual carnival, an event shunned by all believers.

Strangely enough, the partying didn't give Mara the same rush that it had before. Mara had changed more than she thought – changed on the inside. She went back to church and when she was ready, asked to be baptised. This time it felt right.

Mara was a bright student. During her four and a half years at the university she took two degrees in pharmacy and biochemistry. At the same time she attended a Bible School two nights a week for two years. After her studies she could find no work in the city, so returned to her hometown. For the next six years Mara worked part-time in a pharmacy. She dedicated the rest of her time to preaching and teaching in the church, and leading the youth in evangelistic outreaches. Mara thrived under the challenge and often caught herself thinking she'd like to do this for the rest of her life.

Living at home as a Christian, Mara was now more aware of the spiritual battlefield. Sometimes a terrible sound filled her ears, and on several occasions she felt like she was being suffocated. Only crying out for the protection of Jesus' blood brought relief. Mara's mother was less than thrilled with her daughter's conversion, but said she recognized a 'good aura' around her. She even urged her to pray for certain people in need. Mara tried to witness to her family. Over the next several years three of her sisters finally came to faith.

Just when she thought she had found her niche, Mara had another startling dream. This time she was in a country she identified as Germany. The Lord seemed to be saying that he was going to take her there. This made no sense at all. She had never contemplated going to Europe. Why go somewhere that had already heard so much of the gospel, when there were other needy places even in Brazil?

Mara did feel, however, that she should do more to awaken local churches to mission, and helped to organize her own fellowship's first mission conference. The speaker brought a representative from Operation Mobilization, who taught her how to do sketchboard evangelism. He also got her excited about OM's summer campaigns. The next two summers she went on outreach teams in Brazil and Paraguay.

Meanwhile, the dream about Germany surfaced again. Mara began to look into ministries in this country. She also prayed, 'Lord if the dream really was from you, please be patient with me and send it again.'

The third time she had the dream, Mara was convinced. God had been bringing Germany to her attention through various ways for six years. She told him she was ready to trust his direction, and go.

Mara attended OM's orientation conference for new recruits and by faith made plans to leave Brazil early in 1988. She had already started to learn German. She had also managed to raise part of her support through her church and other friends. After this, there seemed no other possible source of income. But God honoured her faith and at the last minute another church unexpectedly supplied the needed balance.

Culture shock was inevitable as Mara flew from a Brazilian summer to a European winter. It was far colder than she imagined. The food was a lot different, too, and of course the biggest hurdle was her imperfect English. But she was content to know she was in the place God wanted her. OM had a ministry among Turks and Kurds in Berlin: immigrants who had not had the chance to respond to the gospel. If God could use her to share his good news among these people, she'd be happy!

Intensive language learning followed the next year. While improving her English, Mara went to a German language school and lived for several months with a Berlin family. In her second year she began learning Turkish. As she adjusted to the various cultures, she threw herself into practising the language and sharing her faith. She began to make friends. Often she was invited into homes and enjoyed the friendly hospitality.

Mara knew that many of her team-mates were preparing for further service in Turkey. Frans Roelofse was one of them. She liked the fair-haired South African, and was surprised at how much she missed him when he went on a short trip to Turkey the first year. That summer they got a chance to know each other better as they were both delegated to lead a special outreach team.

The evening before Frans moved to Turkey, he asked Mara for their first and only 'date'. They liked each other's company and started to exchange letters during the next months. Then Frans wrote that he wasn't sure he wanted to marry a foreigner. Since there probably wasn't any future in their relationship, he suggested they should put all else aside and concentrate on ministry.

Mara was deeply disappointed. She wasn't interested in meaningless dating but she wanted a husband, a partner in ministry. And she had really felt the Lord was telling her that Frans was the one.

Everyone seemed to expect Mara would also go to Turkey. Although she had learned a lot about working with Muslims, she was not at all certain this was God's plan for her. But she decided to ask OM and her church if she could spend some time in Turkey before returning to Brazil.

In 1990 Mara saw history unfolding as the Wall dividing East and West Berlin was torn down in front of her eyes. Soon afterwards she was on her way to Ankara, Turkey. Was she pursuing God's will, or Frans? She had to confess that he still meant a lot to her. But Frans was based in another city, and when he came to see her it was only to say their relationship was over.

Mara's heart sank. On a long walk, she poured out her feelings to the Lord. Then she finally surrendered her own will in the matter. 'From now on,' she promised, 'I will focus wholly on reaching people for you, Lord.'

But the next morning, the Lord seemed to fill her heart and head with a verse she had memorized some time earlier. The words came from Romans 4:17: 'He is our father . . . the God who gives life to the dead and calls things that are not as though they were.'

Mara was bewildered. What did this mean? That God would someday give new life to her 'dead' relationship with Frans? That was the last thing she expected. And living in hope again was just too painful. She tried to push the verse out of her mind.

But six months later God did exactly as he'd promised. As Frans gave himself to a period of intensive prayer about the whole matter, the Lord repeatedly gave him verses that seemed to point to his approval of Mara. The two asked the mission for permission to see more of each other. In February 1991 they visited South Africa so Mara could meet Frans' family. There they got engaged, and were married the following June in Brazil. Her parents slaughtered an ox from the farm and wedding guests celebrated with a traditional *churrasco* (barbecue). By the autumn the newlyweds were back in Turkey and facing the toughest assignment of their lives.

Bursa, located in the north-western part of the country and a few hours from Istanbul, had the distinction of being the biggest city in the world without a church. Various missions had been trying unsuccessfully for years to get a foothold in this conservative Muslim stronghold. Several families had been deported. The Roelofses worked with two other couples in the city but they met only once a week for prayer.

Frans and Mara set to work following up the men and women who had signed up for Bible correspondence courses advertised in newspapers and other places. The correspondence ministry was probably the single most successful instrument for introducing Turks to Jesus since it began in the 1960s. In 1991 alone, nine thousand signed up. Visits to interested students in Bursa and nearby cities had to be carefully arranged so that they would not draw attention. The pair also gave gospels and leaflets to individuals whenever the opportunity occurred, and brought the 'Jesus' video to play on long bus trips.

While Turkey's secular government officially allows freedom of religion, the reality on the streets is quite different. Handing out tracts is a good way to get arrested. Home Bible studies, mostly attended by correspondence study contacts, proved successful, however, with up to thirteen or fourteen attending. Separate men's and women's meetings were also held for discipleship purposes. Unfortunately, two in the group only pretended interest to leak information to the police or fundamentalists. The Roelofses and other leaders started receiving telephone death threats.

Like many Christian workers in Turkey, both Mara and Frans knew what it was to be arrested. Mara was still single and part of an outreach team at an Aegean Sea campground when police detained them for questioning. Fortunately they were released after only a day behind bars.

Mara tried not to let the hate calls disturb her too deeply. Still, it was hard not to look over her shoulder whenever she was out. Was she being followed? Was their phone tapped? She reminded herself of God's faithfulness and claimed his protection. After several months, the informants were identified and confronted.

Mara sought to widen her circle of friends by joining Muslim neighbour ladies in a weekly 'coffee club' that rotated around to each woman's home. She found most of these gatherings very superficial, with talk focusing on food and fashion, but whenever it was her turn she tried to introduce a spiritual note. Sometimes she distributed a verse to each woman and asked God's blessing on the food. Everyone knew that Mara and her husband were Christians so they were tolerant. At Christmas she distributed homemade cookies to neighbours and friends, tucking in cards with Scripture verses.

While women would never ask spiritual questions in a group, Mara sometimes had the opportunity to share on a one-to-one basis. It was even possible to pass on a New Testament *(Injil)*. Once, after giving one to a very conservative Muslim woman, her husband appeared at the door to ask for more.

Observing the popularity of book fairs in the city, Mara suggested trying a Bible stall at the annual fair. The idea proved so successful that the outlet has continued to this date, in spite of regular harassment by police and fundamentalists. In time a small bookshop was opened in one of the shopping areas, staffed by local Christians.

During the summer of 1992, Frans and Mara took part in teams that travelled through Central Asia and Bulgaria, mostly by train. They were thrilled to discover that many people in the newly independent republics were quite open to learning about Jesus Christ. Decades under Communism had left a void that hungered to be filled. The teams showed the Jesus video in Turkmen, Kirgiz and Uzbek languages, and gave out about eight hundred gospels and other literature.

This was the couple's last summer on their own. Early the next year Mara fell pregnant, and they remained in Turkey for the delivery in September. In fact, Leonardo was a few weeks overdue and was delivered by Caesarean section. Although Mara missed having family members around to ease her first weeks of motherhood, she received plenty of advice. The Turkish culture abounds with superstitions about childbirth and parenting. For example, women are warned not to cut their hair when they're pregnant, and small blue amulets are pinned on babies to fend off the 'evil eye'.

Forty days after a child's birth is the traditional consecration day. Turkish mothers usually celebrate this with other women, reading from the Qur'an and singing to the prophet Mohammad. Mara decided to use the day to consecrate Leonardo to the Lord. Inviting fourteen of her women friends, they sang praise songs, and she delivered a sketchboard message and distributed gifts of gospels as part of the festivities.

Leonardo was a happy and healthy baby. Mara and Frans loved him dearly and were pleased to find that having a child allowed them to integrate better into the Turkish culture. Later, as their son grew old enough for kindergarten and then primary school, there were some-times opportunities to give out booklets about Moses, Abraham and Jesus to other parents. These were received with surprising enthusiasm.

Second son Filipe was born at the end of the long, very hot summer of 1995. This time all did not go so smoothly. Mara's doctor noticed the baby didn't breathe normally at delivery, and advised his parents to take him to a leading Ankara hospital to see a heart specialist. The tests showed that Filipe had a small hole in his heart. A few months later, a geneticist confirmed that he also had Down's syndrome.

Their joy over Filipe was now clouded by fear and doubt. What purpose could God have in allowing these disabilities? How could they cope with raising Filipe within Turkey's limited facilities? Their hurt was com-pounded when the doctor in Ankara delicately suggested that they should not tell anyone their son had Down's: people 'just wouldn't understand'.

Mara felt trapped. She told Frans that they must leave the country. Being a mother was stressful enough without this difficulty. Surely they would all be better off living somewhere in the West.

Mara poured her heart out to the Lord. 'Why did this have to happen, God? How are we supposed to handle this?'

'*My grace is sufficient for you,*' she heard him answer. '*Trust me. My strength will be made perfect in your weakness.*'

'Yes, Lord, I know. But what about Filipe? What if living here doesn't work for him, if people are unkind, or we can't meet his needs?'

'*Filipe is my gift to you. Have I not already proven my faithfulness? I will never let him or you or Frans be tested beyond what you can bear. I will provide a way for you to handle every problem.*'

So they took the Lord at his word. They would stay in Turkey for as long as he indicated. They contacted the Down's Syndrome Association in England for advice. 'Share Filipe's condition with everyone,' they urged, 'you need their support and so does he.'

The Roelofses discovered helpful books and videos, and foreign friends in Turkey gave Filipe some educa tional toys. The family travelled to specialists in Istanbul to learn more about occupational, speech and physio-therapy that could help Filipe. They did not find a therapist in Bursa so Mara did exercises with her son for forty-five minutes each day. And as he grew, so did their thankfulness for him, and their confidence that God makes no mistakes.

A year or two later when they were visiting South Africa, it suddenly struck Mara that she had access to many more resources than most parents of Down's children in Turkey. Perhaps God wanted her to help them? If only she could find a professional therapist willing to visit Turkey for a few weeks.

Eventually she located an occupational therapist willing to fly out to Bursa and organize a clinic in their home.

The specialist evaluated each child and gave parents a recommended programme to follow. Mara had already invited mothers to a regular meeting at her home. The ten or so women who came overwhelmed her with their gratitude. No one else understood, they told her. They had always been afraid and ashamed to talk about their children: disabilities were so often regarded as a mark of God's punishment and disfavour. All the ladies received a set of information about Down's syndrome, plus a booklet about the love of Jesus. In time, with input from Mara, Bursa established its own Down's Syndrome Association.

By this time a small church had begun to meet. Although believers were interrogated by police and abused by their families, a core of six to twenty faithful believers were now regularly meeting in an apartment building. Frans helped to lead the fellowship for the first few years until a Turkish pastor was ready for leadership. Mara also did some of the teaching, and discipled the women at separate gatherings. Police harassment continued, however. Soon after the opening of the church, Frans was called in twice by the anti-terror department of the Bursa police, who asked for a list of all the members. Frans refused. He did give the chief the books about their faith that he requested. But the man was obviously antagonistic, and during one evangelistic concert in the church, threatened to close it down.

Almost since the beginning, Frans had held a Turkish work permit as a travel agency representative. This had been a great help in obtaining visas and residence permission. In 1998 he received another two-year extension on this permit. However, the Bursa police opposing his involvement in the church refused Frans the usual residence stamp. Soon afterwards he was notified his work permit had been cancelled. Police arrested him in his office and after two nights in jail, deported him.

Frans was able to re-enter the country after only a day. But for about a year after that he was obliged to exit the country every month to renew a tourist visa from Greece. Mara's Brazilian visa required her to leave every three months. With the children this was quite an upheaval. But Frans opened a court case against the government, declaring religious discrimination, and won. His two-year visa was eventually reinstated.

In August 1999 Turkey was hit with one of the most destructive earthquakes in history. The epicentre was in Izmit, just seventy-five miles north of Bursa. Mara had by this time grown accustomed to occasional tremors. But this night it was different. A roaring sound filled her with dread, and the swaying of the building seemed to go on forever. She held Filipe close and prayed as the quake, measuring 7.8 on the Richter scale, took the lives of over 17,000 people in the area. Aftershocks continued for days. For several nights their family joined the thousands around the city who slept outside their apartment buildings. Frans helped with Operation Mercy relief effort accounts during the next days and weeks. Mara found many opportunities to talk with people about eternity.

Both Leonardo and Filipe were doing well. Leonardo started attending a Turkish school in September that year. In the afternoon of his first school day there was another quake and all the schools in the vicinity were closed for two weeks. But he adapted to his very large class of sixty children and was slowly starting to read. With Mara speaking to him in Portuguese and Frans in Afrikaans, he was growing up trilingual.

Filipe was also making progress, thanks to the faithful speech therapy and physiotherapy that Mara daily practised with him. Tests revealed that the opening in his heart was also slowly closing. Filipe played happily in his Turkish kindergarten. Although he was communicating quite well in Turkish, the Roelofses felt their son would make the best progress in an English speaking school. Since there was no such school in Bursa they were considering a move to the south coast city of Izmir, in 2001. But that summer a few of the teachers in Izmir's Christian school finished their commitment and left, leaving the future in question. Frans and Mara began to explore other options. South Africa was one, but they were anxious to continue a ministry with Turks. OM in Britain had a team in London that was entirely focused on Muslims, with a special branch reaching out to Turks and Kurds. A family like theirs would be a definite asset.

As a London apartment suddenly became available at reasonable cost and other details fell into place, God seemed to be giving Mara and Frans a green light for the move. Leaving Turkey after eleven and a half years was hard. Both had invested so much in the land and people and the church in Bursa was growing. Believers were more established in their faith. Activities like film shows, concerts, seminars and a teahouse in the church were drawing more and more new people. These were exciting times.

England, they knew, would require big adjustments by the whole family. The cost of living was also more. But additional support came from unexpected sources. Advice from the Down's Association lawyer also proved invaluable in covering the expense of a required private speech therapist's report.

England's capital had over a million Muslims worshiping at hundreds of mosques; it didn't take Mara long to realize that she was surrounded by Muslims and Hindus from all over the world. Mara made friends easily, especially with her facility to speak six languages. Before long she started a prayer group for believing mothers in her area, meeting in her home before they went to pick up their children from school. Once, two Muslim women with children in the same school as her boys came to visit Mara. As she shared about Jesus, one had tears in her eyes.

To her surprise, Mara was able to lead five Muslim women to the Lord during her first two years in Britain – more than in all the years she spent in Turkey. Three small fellowships of Turkish and Kurdish believers now meet to worship Jesus in northern London and Mara is a popular speaker at the Turkish ladies' fellowship. She also makes personal visits to encourage and disciple women, as well as to assist them with practical problems.

A drop-in centre for Turks and Kurds unable to speak English is another ministry outlet. Mara sometimes makes phone calls on behalf of immigrants to doctors, landlords, the Department of Home Affairs and others. In 2003 she took a ten-week Christian counselling course to help the many people who seek advice.

Besides regular activities, their team hosts special summer, Christmas and Easter outreaches that draw many international participants. Their goal has also become Fran's and Mara's: to awaken more believers to the world God has brought within their reach. Mara's zeal for sharing Jesus is in no danger of diminishing in England. Her heart goes out to women who are immigrants and asylum seekers. She understands what it is like to be a stranger struggling with new surroundings, customs and language. And she longs to share with these women the hope that has sustained her.

'Fatima,' she says, 'is a good example of how little it takes to impact someone's life.' Fatima had planned to have an abortion until she heard Mara's testimony about the preciousness of all God-given life. Mara helped to arrange a combined baby shower and Bible study for her. Fatima is now happily raising a beautiful baby son.

One day, looking for a piano teacher for Leonardo, Mara knocked on the 'wrong' door on their street. A young Turk opened the door and explained that he lived with two other Turks, including one from Bursa. Mara was delighted about this contact and a few days later had the men over for dinner. Mara and Frans pray for a continuing relationship that will lead to their salvation.

They pray too for little Sevin, an eleven-year-old Kurdish girl, who has a brain tumour. Mara has taken her boys to visit her in the hospital. Sevin met Jesus through the Turkish Fellowship's Sunday School. Although the prognosis is not good, this little girl has the comfort of a friend who will never leave her side.

Mara has discovered that the more she lets herself be used as a channel of God's love, the less likely she is to be anxious about her own personal concerns. She can lose herself because she is secure in her identity. What did it matter that she was born to a Brazilian medium, married to a South African, the mother of children born in Turkey and now living in Britain? 'Home' lies in the epicentre of God's will.

Mara urges other women who question their identity to find it through the one who made them. She would also challenge them to open their eyes to the world at their doorstep. And to discover that missions is not crossing the seas but seeing the cross.

VITAL STATISTICS: Religious slaves

INDIA AND NEPAL

Parents in southern India and Nepal continue to 'marry' their five to seven-year-old daughters to a Hindu god or temple. They hope this will appease the deity or bring favour. In the past these girls, sometimes called *Devadasis*, served as sacred temple slaves or dancers. Once they reached puberty they provided sexual services to any male who was her social superior. Missionary Amy Carmichael dedicated her life to the rescue and care of hundreds of these children.

Today's temple slaves are used until the priests tire of them, and then sold to the highest bidder as child concubines. Eventually the girls (and any children they conceive) are turned out on the streets to survive any way they can. Still 'married to the gods', they may never marry anyone else. Most are forced into brothels, their distinctive bangles and pendants declaring their original status as temple prostitutes.

Although the practice was outlawed by the British over 150 years ago, there are today an estimated 30 000 *Devadasis* in the State of Andhra Pradesh alone. The idea of marrying daughters to the gods is reviving. However, women's groups are campaigning against it and some Christian organizations are offering alternative lifestyles to girls who have been freed.[1]

WEST AFRICA

Thousands of West African girls as young as four years old have also been offered to the gods, as atonement for some offence committed by a relative. *Trokosi* – which literally means *'slave wives of the gods'* – are part of a three hundred year tradition in the Upper Volta region that encompasses Ghana, Nigeria, Benin and Togo. Until the eighteenth century, Fetish Priests accepted livestock as offerings by families who were fearful of retribution by the gods. But then the priests decided a young virgin would be more useful for domestic and sexual purposes.

A slave's term of service is supposed to last from three to five years, depending on the nature of the sin that is being atoned for. However, most families of *Trokosi* cannot afford the price required to buy their daughters back. They are also fearful of the gods' displeasure. If a priest dies, the woman becomes the property of his successor. But if the girl dies without her family redeeming her, they must replace her with another virgin. The cycle can continue for generations.

Trokosi slaves live in inhuman conditions: frequently raped and beaten, given only rags to wear and forced to beg for food, they receive no education or medical attention and work long hours in the priest's fields. They often suffer from ill health. Babies born to the girls must also become slaves to the priest. Those who resist are beaten into submission.[2]

Through the efforts of a private, non-profit agency called International Needs Ghana, many shrines have now stopped the practice of *Trokosi* and 2900 women have been freed and rehabilitated. The Anti-Slavery Society has also succeeded in purchasing the freedom of over 500 slave girls. In 1998 Ghana passed a law banning the practice. However, several thousand girls still remain in slavery. The law is hard to enforce. Some people argue that it is a part of their culture.

Notes

1 Much of the information in this section can be found on
{http://anti-slaverysociety.addr.com/slaverysasia.htm}. Readers
may be particularly interested in 'Child Hierodulic Servitude in
India and Nepal' and 'Traditional Slavery in West Africa'.
2 Nirit Ben-Ari, Africa Recovery, *Afrol News*, 'Liberating Ghanaian
Girls from "Trokosi"', January 2003.

VITAL STATISTICS: Trafficking

Illegal trade in human beings is one of today's fastest-growing and lucrative businesses and the top human rights issue of the twenty-first century. Victims number from 700 000 to 4 million annually. Police statistics indicate that less than 0.5 per cent of these are male. Most females are imported and exported for forced labour or sexual exploitation; many are sold by destitute parents. Others are lured to another country by false promises of legitimate work. Their passports are then confiscated and they become virtual slaves. *Every nation in the world is involved.*

A 'Convention on the Elimination of All Forms of Discrimination Against Women' – often described as an international bill of rights for women – was adopted in 1979 by the UN's General Assembly. Trafficking in women was defined to include: sexual slavery, both in general and by the military, the deception of migrant women, and 'mail order' and false marriages. The Convention proposed that countries should 'take all appropriate measures, including legislation, to suppress all forms of traffic in women and exploitation of prostitution of women.' Those signing the agreement amounted to 174 countries (90 per cent of the UN members).[1]

All nations that ratified this declaration made themselves legally bound to enforce it. Below is a 'progress' report from a selection of countries.

ASIA

Thailand: The Coalition Against Trafficking in Women has estimated that *1 million women* of various nationalities have been trafficked into Thailand.[2] Between 1990 and 1998, 80,000 women and children were taken into the country for prostitution. The highest numbers are from

Burma (10,000 per year), followed by **China** (5000 per year) and **Laos**.[3] Another 10,000 per year come from the former **Soviet Union**.

Three thousand Thai women and children are annually sent to **Cambodia** for prostitution and to **China** for domestic work.[4]

At least *50,000* **Burmese** girls and women are working in Thailand as prostitutes at any one time.

Thailand did not sign the Convention.

China: More than *250,000 women* and *children* are thought to have been the victims of trafficking within China alone. China ratified the Convention in 1980.[5]

Saudi Arabia: In 1998 an airplane full of young **Indian** girls, many of them scarred or maimed, were returned to India from Saudi Arabia. The girls' parents had apparently sold them during a pilgrimage to Mecca, and they were then forced into prostitution.[6]

United Arab Emirates: 19,000 Pakistani children have been trafficked to the UAE.

Approximately 500,000 women are annually trafficked into Western Europe.

EUROPE

Bulgaria: Approximately 10,000 Bulgarian women are currently thought to be victims of international trafficking operations.[7]

Italy: Official Italian statistics reveal that there are approximately 900 child prostitutes in Italy being trafficked from Albania. A total of over 8000 Albanian girls are sent into Italy's sex trade, more than 30 per cent of them under eighteen years.[8]

In Milan, women abducted from the countries of the former **Soviet Union** were auctioned on blocks, and sold at an average price of just under 1000 dollars. Trafficking in women and girls for prostitution and forced labour to Italy is a growing problem. The women and girls are usually from Albania, Nigeria, the former Soviet Union and Eastern Europe.[9]

Greece is increasingly being used as both a destination and transit point for trafficking, with between 16,000 to 20,000 women in the country at any one time. An academic observer estimated that approximately *40,000 women*, most between the ages of twelve and twenty-five, are trafficked to Greece each year for prostitution. *Seventy-five per cent are not told why they are being brought to Greece.*[10]

Germany is a major destination and transit country for trafficked women, with estimated numbers ranging all the way up to *20,000* per year. These are expected to include around 15,000 **Russian** and **Eastern European** women, who are put to work as prostitutes.[11]

Homeless children in *Romania* (which just ratified the Convention in 2003) have increasingly been trafficked under false pretences and forced into prostitution in Berlin and Hamburg, Germany, and Amsterdam.

Great Britain: A Government-sponsored report estimates that up to *1500 women and girls* are trafficked into the country annually for purposes of sexual exploitation, from Eastern Europe and the Balkans, South America, Nigeria, Thailand and Vietnam.[12]

AFRICA
South Africa: A major transit point between the developing world, Europe, the United States and Canada. Trafficking of women and children into forced prostitution has now become the third largest source of profits for organized crime after drugs and guns.[13]

At least 1000 **Mozambican** victims are recruited, transported and exploited every year in South Africa.

SOUTH AMERICA

Brazil: The majority of Brazilian women and girls are exported for the purpose of sexual exploitation to Europe, Japan, Israel and the United States.

Colombia: Interpol estimates 35,000 women are trafficked out of Colombia every year, with estimated profits of 500 million dollars.

Mexico is listed by the UN as the number one centre for the supply of young children to North America. The majority are sent to international paedophile organizations. Most of the children over twelve end up as prostitutes.[14]

NORTH AND CENTRAL AMERICA

Canada: Each week Canada receives about 12 sixteen to thirty-year-old Asian girls and women on visitor's permits. They are then sold to brothel owners in Markham, Scarborough, Toronto and Los Angeles, and forced into 40,000 dollar debt bondage. Vietnamese and Chinese mafia arc expanding operations in brothels in Toronto, Canada, trafficking women from Southeast Asia.

The Dominican Republic traffics the fourth highest number of victims in the world. About 400 smuggling rings are in operation, and they have sent approximately 50,000 females into the overseas sex trade. Girls are often lured into marriages under false pretences, and then sold into prostitution by the 'husband'.

Haiti: UNICEF reports an estimated 4000-plus children are trafficked from Haiti every year, exploited by adults who force them to work and turn over their earnings.

USA: An estimated 50,000 women and children are annually trafficked to the United States. They are primarily used for the sex industry, though they also provide maid services at hotels, peddle trinkets on subways and buses, work in sweatshops and beg. The average age is twenty years old.[15]

Chinese women are being sold into the United States for brothels in New York and North Carolina, then forced to work off 40,000 dollars in debt bondage. Some of the women brought to the States are made to pay the debt for their passage by having sex with up to 500 men.[16]

The United States is the major destination country for *young children* kidnapped and trafficked for adoption by childless couples who are unwilling to wait for a child through legitimate adoption procedures and agencies. The largest source country is Mexico. Mexican children over twelve years of age are kidnapped and trafficked to the United States for child prostitution.[17]

'But this is a people plundered and looted, all of them trapped in pits or hidden away in prisons. They have become plunder with no-one to rescue them.' Is. 42:22

Notes

1 See {http://www.un.org/womennwatch/daw/cedaw/}.
2 Ahmad Saufian and Pusat Kajian Perlindungan Anak, 'Child Labour in Jermals', *Child Workers in Asia*, Vol. 15, No. 2, 1999.
3 ILO-IPEC, 'Combating Trafficking in Children for Labour Exploitation in the Mekong Sub-region', October 1998.
4 ECPAT Bulletin, 'Report Cites Burma's Child Rights Abuses', Vol. 4, No. 1, 1996–97.
5 UNICEF, 'Children on the Edge', citing, 'Every Last Child: Fulfilling the Rights of Women and Children in East Asia and the Pacific', (UNICEF: East Asia and Pacific, 2000).
6 'A Human Rights Report on Trafficking of Persons, Especially Women and Children', The Protection Project, March 2002.
7 US Department of State, 'Country Reports on Human Rights Practices, 1999', 25th February 2000.
8 *CATW Fact Book*, citing G. J. Koja, '8000 Albanian Girls Work as Prostitutes in Italy', HURINet, 25th July 1998.
9 US Department of State, 'Country Reports on Human Rights Practices, 1999'.

10 US Department of State, 'Country Reports on Human Rights Practices, 2001', March 2002.

11 Gillian Caldwell et al., 'Crime and Servitude', Global Survival Network, 1997.

12 US Department of State, 'Trafficking in Persons Report', 12th July 2001.

13 Zurayah Abass, Director of 'Molo Songololo' (a child advocacy group), *BBC News Report*, November 2000.

14 *CATW Fact Book*, citing Allan Hall, *The Scotsman*, 25th August 1998.

15 ILO, Report of the Director General, 'Stopping Forced Labour', Global Report under the Follow-up to the ILO Declaration on Fundamental Principles and Rights at Work, International Labour Conference, 89th Session, 2001, Geneva.

16 *CATW Fact Book*, citing Brad Knickerbocker, 'Prostitution's Pernicious Reach Grows in the US', *Christian Science Monitor*, 23rd October 1996, citing Avita Ramdas of Global Fund for Women.

17 Congressional Research Service Report 98-649 C, May 2000.

VITAL STATISTICS: Widows

When a woman is widowed she becomes a member of one
of the largest and most marginalized of the world's people
groups. All too often the traumatized are also victimized.

**In some countries over 50 per cent of all adult women are
widowed. The numbers are even greater in conflict-torn
regions, or in those hosting large refugee populations.[1]**

AFRICA

**Millions of widows in sub-Saharan Africa are
robbed, beaten, raped and evicted from their homes
– often by their own in-laws – because women are
considered unworthy of equal property rights.
Unlawful treatment is even more common when a
husband dies of Aids.[2]**

Zimbabwe: Over 34 per cent of widows reported that they
had been accused of causing the death of their husbands.
Such women and their children are usually evicted from
their homes and disinherited. Widows are the poorest and
most stigmatized group in the country.

Zambia: As in most other places, widows suffer
discrimination and injustice and are often deprived of
inheritance. Required acts of mourning may include being:

- Forced to crawl around the funeral house or grave of their
  deceased husbands
- Slapped and starved
- Prevented from bathing or changing their clothing for
  days, weeks or a month
- Kept under a blanket until the burial

- Insulted and shouted at with obscenities
- Accused of having killed their husband, and submitted to trial by ordeal
- Stripped half-naked
- Deprived of some or all of their property
- Sexually 'cleansed' (see below); for example, by insisting they have sex with their father-in-law
- Denied custody of their children, even small babies
- Forced to live with in-laws
- Denied freedom of movement for months or even years, a virtual house arrest[3]

In some areas of Africa, widows are forced to undergo sexual rituals in order to keep their property. *'Wife inheritance'* entitles a male relative of the dead husband to take over the widow as a wife, often in a polygamous family. *'Ritual cleansing'* usually involves sex with a social outcast like the village drunk, who is paid by the dead husband's family. This is supposed to cleanse the woman of her husband's evil spirits. Not only is this practice humiliating and degrading but dangerous, often leading to the spread of Aids. Women who fight back are routinely beaten, raped or ostracized.[4] Since the hundreds of thousands of 'cleansers' at work across Africa are obviously spreading disease, some though not all villages have discontinued the practice.

ASIA

Nepal: The most severe form of widow abuse is labelling her a *bokshi* or witch, and holding her responsible for the death of her husband. Such women may be stoned or beaten to death. Other widows – especially in non-urban parts of Nepal – are generally treated as outcasts, and physically abused by the authorities in their communities. In some areas widows are forced to shave their heads and wear

white clothes. In most parts, they are restricted to eating vegetarian food with limits on spices, etc. Widows have to cook for themselves and cannot eat food touched by others.[5]
Sri Lanka: Years of internal fighting in this country have left many thousands of widows. Wives of men who died in the armed forces are only entitled to benefits if they do not marry. Widows also fear that if they remarry, the children by their first husbands will be mistreated. But women without men in this culture are considered abnormal, and they are vulnerable to sexual and economic exploitation.

INDIA: WIDOW BURNING

The Hindu tradition of *sati* or *suttee* – widows throwing themselves or being pushed onto the funeral pyres of their husbands – was outlawed in 1829 after the cruel deaths of thousands of women. However, the practice continued for many years afterward and still does occur very occasionally. In August 2002 a crowd of 5000 gathered to watch the burning to death of a widow in the state of Madhya Pradesh. When police got to the scene they tried to pull her off the fire, but villagers pelted them with rocks so they were forced to retreat. Her fellow-villagers proclaimed themselves to be proud of the event, and believed the sacrifice would help to end a long drought.[6]

After the legal ban on *suttee*, widows in many places were subjected to a ceremony that formally degraded them. Their heads were shaved and they were forbidden the use of personal ornaments.[7] Even today, India's estimated 40 million widows – both Hindu and Muslim – are commonly blamed, shamed and robbed of property rights. Many flee their homes to escape abusive in-laws. In tribal communities, widows may be accused of being a witch and killed. Hindu widows who remarry are frowned upon; the higher the caste or social position, the more restrictions. In some castes *leviratic* marriage is practised and the widow is taken by a brother. The daughters of widows probably face an even bleaker future. With no one to provide a dowry they are married off to almost anyone who will take them, usually older men.

In 2001, after the huge Hindu Kumbh Mela festival that drew millions of worshippers from all over India, families left behind 10 000 elderly widowed mothers and other unwanted relatives. These poor and infirm women survived as best they could from one day to the next, hoping someone would return for them.[8]

CENTRAL ASIA

Afghanistan: Kabul has been called the widows' capital of the world. Between 30,000 and 50,000 women struggle in this city every day to feed and protect their children; hundreds of thousands of women are in the same predicament nationwide. Most have had little education.

Iraq: This country's population is 60 per cent women, and as many as 300,000 are war widows. Several thousand have accepted 'temporary marriages' in order to survive, although there is great shame and social stigma attached (see Vital Statistics: Brides at risk).

'Religion that God our Father accepts as pure and faultless is this: to look after orphans and widows in their distress.'
Jas. 1:27

Notes

1 See {http://www.oneworld.org/empoweringwidows}.
2 'Human Rights Watch' documented the violations of women's property rights like these in a 2003 report called 'Double Standards: Women's Property Rights Violations in Kenya'.
3 See {http://www.oneworld.org/empoweringwidows/ 10countries/zambia.html}.

4 See {http://www.oneworld.org/empoweringwidows/
10countries/zambia.html}.
5 Haram, Neelofar, 'Muslim Widows, a Case Study in Delhi',
March 2002.
6 'Nation Shocked Over Widow Burning', *The Age*, 9th August 2002.
7 J. C. Oman, *The Brahmans, Theists, and Muslims of India* (Delhi,
1973), p.192.
8 *New Indian Express*, 30th January 2001.

Proverbs

Traditional sayings and prayers are part of the fabric of our cultures. Although some of the ones below are no longer in common use, they still reflect deeply rooted attitudes toward women.

'A man loves first his son, then his camel, and then his wife.'

'A woman's heaven is under the feet of her husband.'
Arab Proverbs

'Men are superior to women on account of the qualities with which God has gifted the one above the other, and on account of the outlay they make of their substance for them.'
Qur'an, 4:34

'If a wife dies, it is like a blow on the ankle.
If a husband dies, it is like a blow on the head.'
Punjabi Proverb

'The birth of a girl, grant elsewhere; here, grant a boy.'
Ancient Atharva Veda of India

'Lord, I thank thee that I was not born a woman.'
Part of the morning prayer of the Orthodox Jew

'When an ass climbs a ladder,
we may find wisdom in a woman.'

'A woman, a dog, and a walnut tree,
the more you beat them the better they be.'
Yoruba (Nigeria) Proverbs

'A woman and an invalid man are the same thing.'
Kikuyu (Kenya) Proverb

'She is born a woman because she committed
a thousand sins in the previous world.'
Buddhist Saying

'Women are human but lower than men.'

*'It is the law of nature that women should not be allowed any
will of her own.'*
Confucius, China

Appendix 1

Seven ways to sharpen your world vision

1. Ask God to remove any 'blind spots' you may have developed. Pray that he will open the eyes of your heart, so that you can see the world as he does.
2. Develop your awareness. Form a habit of jotting down world news items from the newspaper, radio or TV, and use them as a springboard for intercessory prayer.
3. Install the Acts 20:20 vision: 'I have taught you publicly and from **house to house**' (emphasis added). Cultivate a friendship with a neighbour, perhaps someone from a different country. You may be surprised at how warmly you are received if you approach others as a learner, genuinely interested in understanding their culture.
4. Stretch your mind and heart. Reach into unknown horizons through articles, books, and TV documentaries. Use prayer guides like *Operation World*. Make a goal of remembering something new each time.
5. Take an active interest in the mission work your church supports. Get to know the missionaries by

reading and praying over their updates. Invite them to your home if you get a chance.

6. Invest some of your hard-earned money in an overseas project. A sure way of focusing your interest!

7. Consider participating in a mission project during one of your holidays. Mission agencies offer a wide variety of fascinating opportunities throughout the year. You'll return home with much more than a tan!

Appendix 2

Useful websites

Each of us can help turn the tide for girls and women caught in the circumstances described in this book. The internet sites listed below represent only a selection of organizations and efforts that exist to give others hope.

Childbirth

Worldwide Fund for Mothers Injured in Childbirth
{http://www.wfmic.org}

Child brides

Help the Child Brides
{www.helpthechildbrides.com}

Child labour

Anti-slavery Society
{http://anti-slaverysociety.addr.com/slaverysasia.htm}

Child Labor Coalition
{http://www.stopchildlabor.org/}

Fields of Hope

{www.fieldsofhope.org}

Deafness

Deaf World Ministries
{http://www.deafworldministries.com}

Silent Blessings
{http://www.silentblessings.org/}

World Federation for the Deaf
{http://www.wfdnews.org/default.php}

Domestic violence

Domestic Violence Data Source
{http://www.domesticviolencedata.org/default.htm}

Female circumcision

Amnesty International
{http://www.amnesty.org/ailib/intcam/femgen/fgm1.
htm}

Equality Now
{http://www.equalitynow.org/}

Girl soldiers

Amnesty International
{http://web.amnesty.org/pages/childsoldiers-index-eng}

Child Soldiers
{www.child-soldiers.org}

Save the Children
{http://www.savethechildren.org/}

Poverty

Food for the Hungry
{http://www.fh.org/}

Food for the Poor
{http://www.foodforthepoor.org/}

The Hunger Site
{http://www.thehungersite.com}

Refugees

Women's Commission for Refugee Women and Children
{http://www.womenscommission.org/}

Worldwide Refugee Information
{www.refugees.org}

Religious slaves

Anti-slavery Society
{http://anti-slaverysociety.addr.com/slaverysasia.htm}

Every Child Ministries
{http://www.thinkwow.com/slavechild/}

International Needs Ghana
{http://www.intneeds.org/trokosi.php}

Street kids

Street Kids for Christ
{http://www.streetkids.net/}

Trafficking

Captive Daughters
{http://captivedaughters.org/}

Coalition Against Trafficking in Women
{http://www.catwinternational.org/}

End Child Prostitution, Pornography and Trafficking of
Children for Sexual Purposes (ECPAT)
{http://www.ecpat.net/}

Global March
{http://www.globalmarch.org/child-trafficking/virtual-
library/trafficking-women.htm}

Human Trafficking
{http://www.humantrafficking.org/}

Violence to Disabled Women

Violence Against Women
{http://www.vaw.umn.edu/}

Widows

Afghan Widows and Orphans Fund
{http://www.awof.org/}

Afghan Women's Association Intl., Widows' Project
{http://www.awai.org/widowproject.html}

Empowering Widows in Development: Ten Country
Report
{http://www.oneworld.org/empoweringwidows/10cou
ntries/}

War Widows International
{http://www.warwidows.org/}

General human rights sites

Human Rights Watch
{http://www.hrw.org/women/index.php}

Open Doors USA: "Women of the Way"
{http://www.opendoorsusa.org/Display.asp?Page=Learn}

Save the Children
{http://www.savethechildren.org/}

United Nations
{http://www.un.org/womenwatch/}

United Nations Development Fund for Women
{www.unifem.org}

What You Need to Know About: Women's Issues
{http://womensissues.about.com/}

Women for Women International
{www.womenforwomen.org}

Appendix 3

Suggested reading

Adeney, Miriam, *Daughters of Islam: Building Bridges with Muslim Women* (Illinois: InterVarsity Press, 2002)

Brooks, Geraldine, *Nine Parts of Desire: The Hidden World of Islamic Women* (London: Hamish Hamilton, 1995)

Ellis, Deborah, *The Breadwinner: A Girl's Life Under Taliban Rule* (Toronto: Groundwood Books, 2001)

Ellis, Deborah, *Parvana's Journey* (Toronto: Groundwood Books, 2003)

Hall, Christine, *Daughters of the Dragon: Women's Lives in Contemporary China* (London: Scarlet Books, 1997)

Hughes, M. Donna, L. J. Sporcic, N. Z. Mendelsohn, and V. Chirgwin, *The Factbook on Global Sexual Exploitation*, published on {http://www.catwinternational.org/fb/} (Coalition Against Trafficking in Women, 1999)

Love, Fran and J. Eckheart (eds), *Ministry to Muslim Women: Longing to Call Them Sisters* (Pasadena: William Carey Library, 2000)

Muhsen, Zana and A. Crofts, *SOLD: One Woman's True Account of Modern Slavery* (London: Time Warner, 1994)

Parshall, Phil and Julie Parshall, *Lifting the Veil: The World of Muslim Women* (Georgia: Gabriel Publishing, 2002)

Rockness, Miriam Huffman, *A Passion for the Impossible: The Life of Lilias Trotter* (Illinois: Harold Shaw Publishers, 1999)

Roper, Matt, *Street Girls: Hope on the Streets of Brazil* (Carlisle: Paternoster Lifestyle, 2001)

Sasson, Jean, *Princess* (New York: William Morrow & Co., 1992)

Sasson, Jean, *Princess Sultana's Daughters* (New York: Doubleday, 1994)

Sasson, Jean, *Desert Royal* (London: Bantam Books, 1999)

Shakib, Siba, *Afghanistan, Where God Only Comes to Weep* (London: Century, 2002)

Stacy, Vivienne, *Women in Islam* (London: Interserve, 1995)